# Vegetarian Cooking

With foreword and
Star Recipes by
Rose Elliot

# HOLLAND & BARRETT

Published exclusively for
Holland and Barrett, Aldwych House,
Madeira Road, West Byfleet,
Surrey KT14 6DA
by Thorsons Publishing Group Ltd,
Wellingborough, Northamptonshire

First published 1986

© THORSONS PUBLISHING GROUP LIMITED 1986

ISBN 0 7225 1330 5

Design, styling and photography by Paul Turner
and Sue Pressley, Stonecastle Graphics,
Tunbridge Wells, Kent

Printed in Italy

STAR RECIPES COURTESY
OF ROSE ELLIOT

# Contents

# Foreword

I was delighted to be asked to write the foreword for this book, and for some of my recipes to be included in the text. More and more people are becoming drawn to the idea of vegetarian cooking, whether for reasons of health, economy or compassion towards animals, or sometimes as a direct result of having tried a really good vegetarian meal at a restaurant or friend's house! Whatever the reason, there seems to be an ever-increasing demand for information about the vegetarian way of cooking and eating, and 'Vegetarian Cooking' provides a helpful introduction to the subject.

A number of myths seems to have grown up about vegetarian cookery. One of these is that vegetarian meals are strange and difficult to plan; another is that you practically need to have a degree in nutrition in order to be healthy on the diet; and yet a third is that the food is complicated and time-consuming to make. Needless to say, all these ideas are completely wrong!

Planning vegetarian meals is no more difficult than planning 'meat-and-two-veg' meals. At its simplest level, you can simply replace the meat part of the meal with a vegetarian dish containing cheese, egg, nut or pulse protein; this book offers a number of delicious suggestions. Don't forget, though, that a number of your favourite recipes may already be 'unconsciously vegetarian': things like quiches, pizza, stuffed jacket potatoes or cheesey potato bakes. Serve these favourites more often, add some new (especially bean and pulse) recipes, and you'll find you soon get into the hang of planning and cooking vegetarian meals.

On the nutritional side, as this book points out, there is no problem whatever about getting enough protein on a vegetarian diet. Do not take any notice of people who say that vegetarian proteins, that is beans, nuts, seeds and grains, are 'incomplete' and have to be balanced and complemented in order to be nutritious. This popular myth is based on a misunderstanding of an idea expressed in an American book called 'Diet for A Small Planet'. The author, Frances Moore Lappe, has since clarified and explained the matter, but unfortunately the myth of incomplete proteins lingers on.

What you do need to watch in a vegetarian diet is your sources of B vitamins. But you're fine here if you include wholemeal bread and whole grains (such as brown rice) in your meals and use a yeast extract in your cooking and/or on bread. Wheatgerm is another food to include, perhaps sprinkled over breakfast cereals, and a daily 'dose' of brewer's yeast (a rounded teaspoonful) or some yeast tablets are a very good idea (and something, incidentally, that many meat-eaters would benefit from, too). A vitamin D supplement is also recommended, especially for children: and this, too, applies to meat-eaters as well.

Regarding the belief that vegetarian cookery is complicated and time-consuming, this is not so. If it were, I, for one, would not be able to contemplate it! I also have two student daughters who do not have much time (or money) for making meals, but both (along with many other students) find vegetarian cooking perfectly practical in cramped conditions and without the labour-saving equipment to which they've been accustomed at home! Indeed, vegetarian cookery, like just about any other kind, can be as simple or as complicated as you want to make it.

There are many fast vegetarian dishes such as pasta with tomato sauce and grated cheese; brown rice with stir-fried vegetables or a quickly-made ratatouille; thick lentil soup with wholemeal rolls or garlic bread; vegetables in a cheese sauce; toasted cheese sandwiches (or baked beans on toast) with salad; and the lazy gnocchi, potato cakes and speedy burgers from the cooker top and grill section of this book, to mention just a few. In addition, most vegetarian burgers, bakes and savoury loaves freeze extremely well and it may be worth freezing some one-portion batches if there's just one vegetarian in the family. As mentioned in this book, it's also a great help to cook a double batch of ingredients such as brown rice and then use them as the basis of two completely different dishes. For instance, to half your batch you can add skinned and chopped tomatoes, fried onions and steamed carrots and green beans, to make a vegetable rissotto one day, then mix the remainder with fried onion, tomato, walnuts and basil, and use to fill green or red peppers, topping with grated cheese and serving with a cheese sauce.

Incidentally, if you find you're relying rather heavily on cheese for main meals, just make sure that your other two meals of the day are low in fat, with a breakfast based on wholegrain cereals, fruit and/or low fat yoghurt, and a light meal with grain, yoghurt, low-fat cottage cheese, pulse or nut protein (such as peanut butter and salad sandwiches, lentil soup and salad, or hummus with salad and pitta breads, or baked beans on toast) to redress the balance, and try and include bean and pulses (cooked, or sprouted) in your main meals as often as you can, both because of their low fat content and the important minerals and vitamins which they contain.

I hope that these pointers, and the recipes and tips which follow in this book, will help to make your vegetarian cooking enjoyable and practical for your life-style. If you've been wondering whether to take the plunge, or to try more meatless dishes, hesitate no longer! Look through this book, buy a few ingredients and start to enjoy the delicious flavours and many health benefits of vegetarian cooking today! I wish you the very best of luck.

# Question-time

An increased interest in healthy eating habits is starting to show itself, either instinctively, or in response to more media coverage in the wake of various Government reports on the nation's health. We are being urged for our health's sake to eat substantially less fat, especially of the saturated variety, less sugar and salt, and much more fibre in the form of wholegrains and fresh fruit and vegetables. A well-balanced vegetarian diet meets these requirements admirably and even confirmed meat-eaters will benefit from incorporating many more vegetarian dishes into their day-to-day diet. This book is aimed to help you do just that as well as answer some of your questions on the subject of vegetarianism.

---

## What exactly is a vegetarian diet?

In effect, it is one which omits meat and meat-derived products (lard, dripping, suet, gelatine, etc), poultry and usually fish but includes a limited amount of dairy produce and eggs. A vegan diet is more restrictive and avoids animal produce as well.

---

## Is it healthy?

A well-balanced vegetarian diet can be a very healthy way of eating. It should be based on fresh fruits and vegetables, wholegrains including wholewheat bread, nuts and pulses (dried peas, beans and lentils), seeds, and a certain amount of dairy produce and eggs.

---

## Does the vegetarian diet lack protein?

Ample is provided by wholegrains, including wholewheat bread, and potatoes, vegetables and fruit alone. If concentrated sources including pulses, nuts, seeds and dairy produce are also eaten, then more than enough is supplied.

## What about other essential nutrients?

Iron is supplied by dried fruits (apricots, peaches, figs, dates, raisins and prunes, etc), wholegrain cereals, nuts especially almonds and cashews, bananas, potatoes, leafy green vegetables, molasses, brewer's yeast, prune juice.

Calcium is found in cheese, yoghurt, milk, soya beans and flour, almonds, brazils, hazelnuts, sunflower and sesame seeds and sesame cream (tahini), dried figs, broccoli, parsley and watercress.

Wholegrain cereals, wheatgerm, sunflower seeds, fresh and dried fruits, vegetables and pulses contain other essential minerals and B vitamins, but brewer's yeast and yeast extract make useful supplements.

Sunlight on skin and some fortified margarines supply vitamin D and the main sources of iodine for vegetarians and vegans are seaweed and its various products like vegetarian jelling agents (agar agar and gelozone). Kelp can also be taken in powder or tablet form or use a kelp-based seasoning powder instead of salt.

## How can I plan a balanced diet?

The best way to plan the major meal of the day is to choose a protein-based main dish, adding potatoes cooked in their skin, or brown rice, or wholewheat bread as required with lightly-cooked green and root vegetables or salad and fresh fruit or a low fat/low sugar pudding if needed. Breakfast can be based on a variety of wholegrains, fresh fruits and yoghurt, whilst the remaining meal can be of salad or a warming soup with suitable additions.

# Daily Meal Plan

## Breakfast

- Fresh fruit or dried fruit compote, *or*
- Wholegrain cereals (muesli, granola, wheat germ, etc) or porridge with added nuts and seeds, fresh or dried fruit, skimmed milk or yoghurt or fruit juice to moisten, *or*
- Wholewheat bread or toast and honey or sugar-free jam, or grilled tomatoes, or mushrooms, or baked beans, or yeast extract or the occasional egg.

## Lunch or Light Evening Meal

Varied salad of shredded, chopped or sliced leaf and root vegetables and fruit such as apples, bean and seed sprouts, chopped fresh herbs, with a suitable dressing and two of these basic proteins — nuts, pulses or cereal grains. Fresh fruit or additive-free low fat plain or fruit yoghurt for dessert.

## Main Evening (or Midday) Meal

Make the main meal a protein one basing it on eggs, cheese or a vegetarian-style savoury dish which combines two of the three plant proteins — nuts, grains or pulses. This includes brown rice dishes like paella, risotto, curry or rice-stuffed vegetables; pulses and nuts made into roasts and bakes, pâtés, vegetable stuffings, burgers, rissoles, etc. Grains include wholewheat pasta and wholewheat pastry for delicious quiches, pies and pastries. Serve with a raw vegetable salad or lightly-steamed vegetables, including leafy green vegetables if not eaten at the other meal. For dessert: fresh fruit, additive-free low fat plain or fruit yoghurt, or light puddings with wholefood ingredients like those in the Desserts and Baking sections.

## Drinks

Diluted fresh fruit and vegetable juices, mineral water, herb teas, coffee substitutes or drinks made from yeast extract make healthful additions to the diet.

## Is a vegetarian diet more expensive?

In fact, most people find a vegetarian diet works out more cheaply. The main difference will lie in the money meat-eaters spend on meat and fish which vegetarians will spend on cheese, pulses and nuts which are just as filling and nutritious but work out considerably cheaper kilo for kilo or pound for pound.

## Will I need any special kitchen equipment?

Not necessarily! A liquidizer is wonderfully speedy for preparing soups, purees and dips. A food processor has a multitude of functions which could be helpful. A round spring chopper (like the Maxichop) is good for chopping nuts, onions, cabbage and other vegetables. A pressure cooker is superb for speeding up the cooking of beans and pulses — but many people will already have some or all of these items and could manage without the others.

## Must I spend longer in the kitchen?

It's all a matter of organization and planning. Working out menus for a week or so in advance can help reduce shopping trips to a minimum and remind you to cook extra of certain items like brown rice and pulses to use as the basis for several meals as they keep for three or four days in the fridge. Many vegetarian dishes freeze well so cook double or treble portions of family favourites for future use. Remember that dishes like loaves can be served hot with vegetables and gravy one day and cold with salad the next.

Keep a stock cupboard of all the non-perishable items and look for the increasing number of good quality, low additive canned items like tomatoes, and an increasing number of the pulses like red kidney beans, chick peas and so on which can be used for speedy meals.

# A to Z of Herbs and Spices

Used for flavouring and to improve the taste of a whole gamut of dishes, some herbs such as sage and thyme also aid the digestion and other flavourings like pepper stimulate the appetite. They are especially useful in the vegetarian diet as they blend very well with the natural flavours of nuts, pulses and vegetables.

There is nothing quite like the flavour of fresh herbs so do plant some if you have room, even just in a window-box or pots on the kitchen window ledge. Parsley, mint and chives are perhaps the most useful and much better fresh and others can be added later. Freeze any surplus crops and they will be easy to crumble into various dishes.

## Herbs

### Basil

Use fresh or dried (which has a good flavour). It is sweet and pungent so just use a pinch especially in tomato dishes (it is called the 'tomato herb' because it brings out their flavour so well). Also good with salads and vegetables.

### Bay Leaf

Use fresh from the tree or as whole dried leaves (dried ground leaves are not so flavourful). Strong spicy flavour is good for stocks, soups, stews, casseroles, and in savoury sauces. It is an essential part of bouquet garni. Remember to remove before serving!

## Bouquet Garni

A bundle of sweet herbs — usually bay leaf, thyme and a few sprigs of parsley — which can be used fresh or bought dried to give a lovely flavour to stocks, soups, stews and casseroles. Always remove before serving!

## Chervil

Like parsley, although its flavour is more delicate, use this generously in clear vegetable soup, other soups and omelettes.

## Chives

With a mild, onion-like flavour, chives resemble hollow grass and are best used fresh, either chopped or scissor-snipped into sauces, over baked or mashed potatoes, scrambled eggs, omelettes, with cream or cottage cheese, or used as a garnish for egg dishes, salads especially potato, and soups.

## Garlic

Choose hard bulbs and separate into 'cloves'. Also available as powder, granules or salt, garlic has a very strong and distinctive flavour and aroma and boasts antiseptic properties. For a milder taste, wipe round salad bowl or casserole dish with a cut clove; for a stronger effect, chop peeled clove then crush with salt — it is ready when the juice and flesh are clear. Good for tomato and cheese dishes and in salads and dressings but be careful not to overpower the delicate flavour of nuts and vegetables. It is delicious made into garlic butter and served with hot wholewheat bread.

## Marjoram

Available fresh or dried (stronger) with a very fragrant, spicy and powerful flavour. Use sparingly in nut and mushroom dishes, stuffings, with lentils, soups, stews, pizzas, rissoles or omelettes.

## Mint

Add chopped fresh mint to salads, dressings, fresh fruit salads and drinks — also to the cooking water of such vegetables as peas and new potatoes. Can be used as a sauce or for mint butter for vegetables. It does not blend well with other herbs.

## Mixed Herbs

A combination of dried herbs including marjoram or oregano, parsley, sage, thyme and tarragon and used in the same way as bouquet garni, adding flavour to many savouries, especially nut roasts, and good in soups and stews.

## Oregano

This is wild marjoram and it keeps its aroma when dried. Its strong flavour is reminiscent of Italian cookery — use in tomato dishes, pizza, lasagne, salads and salad dressings.

## Rosemary

Available fresh or dried (but better fresh) with a strongly aromatic, camphor-like flavour, rosemary is popular with canned nutmeats; a little fresh makes an unusual addition to salads particularly those with grated carrot, and a pinch gives a delicate flavour to stews but be careful as it can overpower other herbs.

## Sage

Available fresh or dried (has a good flavour), its strong character is good in nutmeats, stuffings, and a little chopped fresh sage makes an unusual addition to salads and egg dishes. Mix with cream cheese for a tasty spread.

## Summer Savory

Known as the 'bean herb', summer savory makes an excellent addition to any bean or pulse dish.

## Tarragon

Available fresh or dried (not so good), its strong flavour goes with egg dishes very well or use chopped fresh in salads, hollandaise sauce and with asparagus dishes. It is also used with wine vinegar for salad dressings.

## Thyme

Available fresh or dried (good flavour) with a strong, sharpish taste — use sparingly to avoid overpowering other flavours. Use for stuffings, nut savouries, stocks, soups, vegetables especially tomatoes, potatoes and courgettes. Add a pinch to gravies or use chopped fresh thyme with salads. Thyme is often used with marjoram or rosemary and is an essential ingredient of bouquet garni.

# Spices

These are the most useful spices for the stock cupboard.

## Caraway Seed

Use in tomato soups and sauces and sprinkled over loaves or halved potatoes while baking.

## Cayenne Pepper

Use sparingly in cheese dishes or mixed with cream cheese as a spread.

## Celery Seed

Gives a delicate celery flavour to nutmeats, rissoles, soups, sauces, casseroles and gravies.

## Cinnamon

Lovely with apples, rhubarb and other sweet dishes.

## Cloves

Their strong, aromatic spicy taste makes them a good addition to soups, bread sauces and other sauces, studded into a piece of onion for easy removal and extra flavour. They are also excellent for apple and pear dishes or in ground form for cakes, milk puddings and mincemeat.

## Coriander Seed

Tie seeds in a piece of muslin for easy removal before serving and use to give flavour to onion, celery or pea soup, curries, and apple or celery dishes.

## Curry Powder

Usually a hot and spicy combination of pepper, chilli, cardamon, cayenne, coriander, cumin, fenugreek, ginger, mustard seed, turmeric, mace and clove! As well as the common use, a pinch adds spice to gravies, egg or vegetable dishes or soups.

## Dill

Use with cashew nut dishes, or try with cucumber, tomatoes or potatoes.

## Ginger

Powdered or grated whole root gives a hot sweet aromatic flavour to stews, casseroles, vegetable soups, cheese dishes, chutneys and pickles, stewed fruit, cakes and biscuits. An essential ingredient of curry powder.

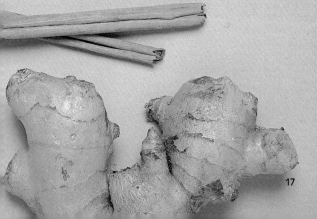

## Ground Mace

Use a pinch in white sauces or with white nutmeats.

## Mixed Spice

This is a ground dried combination of spices, including cinnamon, cloves and allspice, a good substitute for the separate spices and it can be used to flavour puddings, cakes, stewed fruit, crumbles, pies and biscuits.

## Mustard

Hottest in dried powdered form, add a pinch to cheese dishes, salad dressings and sauces.

## Nutmeg

Use freshly grated if possible but the ground type is easier to use. Its sweet spicy taste improves the flavour of creamed or mashed potatoes, sprouts, cabbage, spinach, creamed root vegetables especially carrots, egg custards, nut savouries, puddings, cakes, biscuits, casseroles, pies or sprinkle onto soups.

## Paprika

An attractive and colourful (reddish) garnish for pale-looking dishes like mashed or creamed potatoes, swede or turnip, creamy-coloured soups, cheese dishes, etc.

## Pepper

Freshly-ground black pepper has the best flavour and has health-giving properties lacking in white pepper.

## Salt

Use sea salt, biochemic salt, low-sodium salt substitutes in preference to ordinary table salt.

## Turmeric

This gives a delicious flavour to curries and is a delicate golden colour.

# Soups

As a meal in itself, a snack or a starter to a more elaborate main meal, soup is the perfect choice. Light and delicate, or chilled for a change for warm summer days or chunky and filling for colder weather, there is a soup for every occasion. Liquidizers are a boon for the soup-maker, especially for the lighter soups made from pureed vegetables or for chilled soups, although a most acceptable soup can be made from just a tasty vegetable stock with finely chopped vegetables added.

Chopped fresh green herbs, especially chives, mint or parsley, make an attractive garnish especially for light-coloured or tomato soup, otherwise a swirl of slightly-thinned low fat soft cheese or yoghurt, or a scattering of crispy cubed wholewheat toast or crunchy croûtons add the finishing touch.

## Easy Tomato

| |
|---|
| 1 onion, peeled and chopped |
| 350g (12 oz) potatoes, peeled and diced |
| 1 tbsp oil |
| 425g (15 oz) can tomatoes or 450g (1 lb) fresh |
| 1.2L (2 pts) water |
| Sea salt; freshly ground black pepper |
| Dash of honey |
| Chopped parsley or chives |

Fry onion and potato in oil in a fairly large saucepan for about 5 minutes, stirring often, but don't let them brown. Add tomatoes and water, bring to the boil, then leave to simmer for 15-20 minutes until potato is cooked. Liquidize soup (sieve afterwards if using fresh tomatoes to remove any skin) and return to rinsed-out saucepan, heating gently.

Season with salt, pepper and a little honey if required. Serve with a little fresh parsley or chives snipped over the top.

**Approx. preparation and cooking time:** 40 minutes.

# ☆ Watercress Soup ☆

| Serves 6 |
|---|
| **2 bunches watercress** |
| **1 onion** |
| **450g (1 lb) potatoes** |
| **25g (1 oz) butter** |
| **575ml (1 pt) water** |
| **275ml (½ pt) milk** |
| **Sea salt** |
| **150ml (5 fl oz) single cream or top of milk** |

Wash the watercress carefully, then separate the tough stalks from the leaves; chop the stalks roughly. Peel and slice onion and potatoes. Melt butter in a large saucepan and add the onion; cook gently for 5 minutes without browning, put in potato and watercress stalks (reserving leaves for later). Stir vegetables over a gentle heat for a minute or two to coat with butter then pour in water and milk. Bring mixture to the boil and let it simmer gently for about 15 minutes or until potato is soft. Put soup in liquidizer goblet together with most of the watercress leaves (saving some for garnish) and a little salt and blend until smooth. Stir in cream or top of milk and check seasoning; reheat gently. Divide into serving bowls and decorate with remaining watercress leaves. If you wish to make an everyday version of the soup without the cream, just increase quantity of milk to 400ml (¾ pt).

**Approx. preparation and cooking time:** 45 minutes.

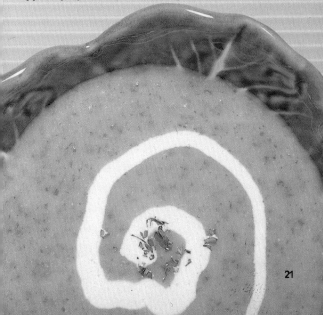

# Carrot Soup

| |
|---|
| **2 large carrots** |
| **1 onion** |
| **25g (1 oz) margarine** |
| **½ tsp thyme** |
| **1 tbsp plain flour** |
| **850ml (1½ pts) water** |
| **Pinch nutmeg** |
| **Sea salt; freshly ground black pepper** |
| **Chopped parsley** |

Scrape and chop carrots; peel and chop onion. Cook in margarine with thyme for 5 minutes but do not brown. Stir in flour and add water. Cook for 30 minutes then liquidize or pass through a sieve or mouli. Season with nutmeg, salt and pepper. Add chopped parsley to garnish.

   For an instant soup, save cooked carrot and onion from a previous meal.

**Approx. preparation and cooking time:** 40 minutes.

# Pea Soup

| |
|---|
| **1 large can garden peas** |
| **1 large onion** |
| **3 cloves** |
| **6 sprigs fresh mint (or use dried)** |
| **850ml (1½ pts) water or stock** |
| **Sea salt; freshly ground black pepper** |
| **Sugar** |
| **Dash of cider vinegar** |

Tip peas into pan. Add onion (peeled) with cloves stuck into it, the mint and water or vegetable stock. Cook until onion is tender. Pass through sieve or mouli, or put into a liquidizer. Flavour with salt and pepper, and sugar if needed. Add a dash of cider vinegar.

**Approx. preparation and cooking time:** 35 minutes.

# Mushroom Soup

| |
|---|
| **225g (8 oz) mushrooms** |
| **Small piece of onion, peeled** |
| **1 bay leaf** |
| **1 garlic clove, peeled and sliced** |
| **A few parsley stalks** |
| **575ml (1 pt) stock** |
| **50g (2 oz) butter** |
| **40g (1½ oz) flour** |
| **About 575ml (1 pt) milk** |
| **Sea salt: freshly ground black pepper** |
| **Nutmeg** |
| **Cayenne pepper** |
| **1 tbsp sherry (opt.)** |

Wash mushrooms and remove stalks. If using field mushrooms, take off skins as well (not necessary with cultivated mushrooms). Put stalks (and skins) into a medium-sized saucepan together with onion, bay leaf, garlic, parsley stalks and stock and bring to the boil, then leave to simmer for 10 minutes to extract the flavours. Strain liquid into measuring jug and make up quantity to 850ml (1½ pts) with the milk.

Melt three-quarters of the butter in the saucepan and stir in flour. When it looks bubbly, pour in a quarter of the milk mixture and stir over fairly high heat until thickened. Repeat process with rest of milk in three more batches. Chop or slice the mushrooms, fry lightly in remaining butter and add to thickened milk with salt, pepper, grating of nutmeg, pinch of cayenne pepper and sherry if using it. Let soup simmer for 3-4 minutes to give flavours chance to blend before serving.

**Approx. preparation and cooking time:** 40 minutes.

# Cauliflower & Fennel Soup

| |
|---|
| **675g (1½ lbs) cauliflower** |
| **175g (6 oz) fennel, diced** |
| **1 tbsp sunflower oil** |
| **1 tbsp wholewheat flour** |
| **1 tsp ready-made mustard** |
| **1 vegetable bouillon (stock) cube** |

## Pastry lid:

| |
|---|
| **100g (4 oz) wholewheat flour** |
| **25g (1 oz) soft vegetable margarine** |
| **25g (1 oz) mature English Cheddar, grated** |
| **1 tsp fennel seeds** |
| **beaten egg to glaze** |

Wash cauliflower, place whole head in saucepan with 5cm (2 inches) boiling water in base. Cover and leave to cook for 10 minutes. Meanwhile set oven to 400°F (200°C), gas mark 6. Sweat fennel and onion in oil for 5 minutes in a heavy-based saucepan. Stir in flour and mustard to coat. Gradually add water from cooked cauliflower to make a smooth sauce. Place cauliflower and sauce on one side to cool. Roughly chop cauliflower and liquidize with fennel and onion mixture. Return to saucepan, thinning, if necessary, with stock.

Make pastry by sieving flour into mixing bowl, adding margarine and rub until mixture resembles breadcrumbs. Stir in fennel seeds and cheese, bind with cold water and roll out. Cut out lids using tops of ovenproof soup bowl or ramekin as cutter.

Pour soup into bowls and glaze inside edge of pastry lid to help it stick to bowl rim. Place in position and glaze top. Bake at once for 15-20 minutes until pastry is golden brown.

**Approx. preparation and cooking time:** 45 minutes.

# Celery Soup

| |
|---|
| **25g (1 oz) margarine or butter** |
| **1 small onion** |
| **6 outside sticks from 1 head of celery** |
| **½ level teaspoon celery seed** |
| **½ level tsp. coriander seed (opt.)** |
| **1 level tbsp. cornflour** |
| **850ml (1½ pts) water or stock** |
| **150ml (¼ pt) top of milk or single cream** |

Melt butter or margarine over a gentle heat. Peel and chop the onion. Wash and dice celery including any leaves and toss gently in the butter or margarine. Cook for 5 minutes, then stir in the flour. Add water or stock and celery seed and coriander seed tied in a piece of muslin. Cook for 45 minutes. Remove muslin bag and liquidize, add seasoning to taste and the top of the milk or cream. Return to heat but do not allow to boil. Serve immediately, garnished with a fresh sprig of parsley.

**Approx. preparation and cooking time:** 1 hour.

# Chilled Cucumber Soup

| 1 cucumber |
| 425g (15 fl oz) natural yoghurt |
| 8 sprigs mint |
| 4 sprigs parsley |
| 1 tsp sea salt |
| 4 sprigs mint to garnish |

Peel cucumber and cut into rough chunks. Put chunks into liquidizer goblet with the yoghurt. Wash mint and parsley and remove stalks. Add leaves to the cucumber and yoghurt together with salt. Blend at medium speed until smoothly pureed. Transfer puree to a bowl and place in fridge until really cold. Check seasoning and add more salt if necessary as chilling tends to dull the flavour, then serve the soup in individual bowls with a sprig of mint floating on top of each.

**Approx. preparation and cooking time:** 10 minutes.


# Onion Soup

| 770g (1½ lbs) onions |
| 40g (1½ oz) butter |
| 1 tbsp flour |
| 850ml (1½ pts) vegetable stock or water |
| 3 tbsp cheap sherry |
| Sea salt; freshly ground black pepper |
| Slices of wholewheat bread |
| 125-175g (4-6 oz) grated cheese |

Peel onions and slice into fairly fine rings. Melt butter in a large saucepan and fry onions for 15-20 minutes until they're golden, stirring now and then, mix in flour and cook for a few seconds before adding stock or water, sherry and a seasoning of salt and pepper. Bring mixture to boil then let it simmer gently with lid on saucepan for 30 minutes. Just before soup is ready, warm heatproof soup bowls and lightly toast slice of bread for each; roughly break toast into bowls. Prepare a moderately hot grill. When soup is ready, check seasoning then ladle into bowls, scatter grated cheese on top and place bowls under grill to melt cheese. Serve immediately.

**Approx. preparation and cooking time:** 55 minutes.

# Winter Vegetable Soup

| |
|---|
| **1.2L (2 pts) water** |
| **2 large carrots** |
| **2 onions** |
| **2 medium-sized potatoes** |
| **1 swede (approx. 225g or 8 oz)** |
| **1 turnip (approx. 225g or 8 oz)** |
| **4 sticks celery** |
| **15g (½ oz) polyunsaturated vegetable margarine** |
| **Sea salt; freshly ground black pepper** |

Put water into large saucepan and bring to boil while preparing vegetables, cutting them into fairly small chunks. Add to water with a little salt and simmer gently with lid on saucepan, until they are all tender — about 30 minutes.

Scoop out 2 big ladlefuls of soup and liquidize or mouli it with margarine, then pour back into saucepan and stir into rest of soup. This thickens the soup, while the pieces of whole vegetable give it body and interest. Check seasoning, adding more salt if necessary and grinding in some black pepper, then reheat soup before serving.

**Approx. preparation and cooking time:** 40 minutes.

# Dips and Starters

Vegetables and pulses make excellent dips and starters — often inexpensive to prepare and not too filling, they can make an excellent contrast to the main meal in appearance, ingredients and method of cooking and are popular with vegetarians and meat-eaters alike. They can also supply extra or complementary protein to balance the rest of the meal when needed.

The recipes are also suitable for buffet dishes or as snacks and some make good sandwich or pitta fillings with chopped salad added.

## Avocado Dip

| Serves 6 |
| --- |
| 250g (8 oz) fromage blanc* |
| 1 clove garlic, crushed |
| 2 large, ripe avocados |
| 1 tbsp lemon juice |
| A little wine vinegar |
| Sea salt; pepper; tabasco |

Mix together fromage blanc, garlic, a little salt, pepper and tabasco. Just before serving, peel and mash the avocados with the lemon juice; add to the creamy cheese, mixing well. Check seasoning, adding a dash of wine vinegar.

Serve with crisp wholewheat toast or crudités.

**Approx. preparation and cooking time:** 10 minutes.

*Fromage blanc is a light smooth cheese like a cross between natural yoghurt and curd cheese with a flavour similar to soured cream.

# Tahini

| |
|---|
| **225g (8 oz) toasted sesame seeds** |
| **½ cup oil (preferably olive)** |
| **2 cloves garlic** |
| **1 tsp sea salt** |
| **Juice of 2 lemons** |
| **½ tsp coriander seeds** |

If using blender, place all ingredients in the goblet with extra water if 1 cup is not sufficient for your machine. Blend until creamy.

To make Tahini by hand use a ridged Japanese mortar (*suribachi*) or place the seeds in a thick polythene bag and crush with a heavy blunt instrument. Transfer seeds to bowl, add rest of ingredients, crushing the garlic separately. Add enough water to make a creamy consistency.

Tahini can be varied by using different spices such as cumin, paprika or parsley. Preparation time: 1 minute with blender, 20 minutes by hand.

**Approx. preparation time:** 5-10 minutes.

# Black Olive Pâté

| |
|---|
| **450g (1 lb) black olives, pitted** |
| **Sea salt (opt.)** |
| **1 tbsp olive oil** |
| **1 clove garlic, crushed** |
| **1 free-range egg, hard-boiled** |

Place all the ingredients in a liquidizer and blend until smooth. Pot, and decorate the top with finely-chopped hard-boiled egg.

Serve with crudités of complementary colours, such as white fennel, cauliflower and chicory leaves, or use as a spread for hot wholewheat toast (butter or margarine is not necessary) and eat with a side salad.

**Approx. preparation time:** 5 minutes.

# Mushrooms à la Grecque

| |
|---|
| **450g (1 lb) small white button mushrooms** |
| **4 tbsp olive oil** |
| **2 tsp ground coriander** |
| **1 bay leaf** |
| **2 garlic cloves, peeled and crushed** |
| **2 tbsp lemon juice** |
| **Sea salt; freshly ground black pepper** |
| **Lettuce leaves** |
| **Fresh parsley** |

Wash mushrooms, halving or quartering any larger ones, then fry in olive oil with coriander, bay leaf and garlic for about 2 minutes, stirring all the time. Turn mushrooms straight into a large bowl to prevent further cooking then add the lemon juice and a grinding of black pepper. Leave mixture to cool, then chill. Check seasoning before serving the mushrooms piled up on lettuce leaves on individual plates, sprinkled with chopped parsley.

**Approx. preparation and cooking time:** 10 minutes.

# ☆ Carrot Terrine ☆

## Mousse

| |
|---|
| 900g (2 lb) carrots |
| 225g (8 oz) parsnips |
| 1 tbsp wholewheat flour |
| 1 tbsp unsalted butter or soft vegetable margarine |
| 150ml (¼ pt) vegetable stock |
| 2 free range eggs, separated |

## Filling

| |
|---|
| 100g (4 oz) spinach |
| Knob of butter or soft vegetable margarine |
| Grated nutmeg |
| 50g (2 oz) low-fat soft cheese |
| 1 leek |
| 1 slice pumpkin |

Steam carrots and parsnips until just cooked. Remove from heat and drain. Make roux by stirring butter and flour together over low heat in heavy-based saucepan. Gradually add stock, stirring well to avoid lumps. Remove from heat and stir in egg yolks. When vegetables are cooked, purée them and stir into roux. Whisk egg whites and add to mixture just before filling terrine.

To make filling, put well-washed spinach in saucepan with knob of butter and grated nutmeg. Cover and cook for 3 minutes. Remove from heat and stir in cheese when cool.

To make terrine: Cut leek and pumpkin into julienne strips. Line 26cm (10½ inch) terrine tin with greaseproof paper. Place layer of carrot mousse in base. Arrange three rows of pumpkin along length of terrine. Cover with thin layer of carrot mousse. Place two or three rows of leek along length of terrine. Cover again with thin layer of mousse. Place spinach filling in piping bag with 1cm (½ inch) nozzle. Pipe two rows of filling along length of terrine and cover with rest of mousse.

Bake at 350°F (180°C) gas mark 4 for 1 hour. If using terrine tin, place dish of water on shelf below to prevent vegetables drying out. If using ceramic or cast iron terrine, place in *bain marie* (dish of water). High in fibre, low in fat.

**Approx. preparation and cooking time:** 1½ hours.

# Hummus

| Serves 8 as a starter |
|---|
| **225g (8 oz) chick peas** |
| **8 tbsp olive oil** |
| **3 garlic cloves, peeled and crushed** |
| **4 tbsp lemon juice** |
| **4 tbsp sesame cream (*tahini*)** |
| **Sea salt** |
| **Paprika pepper** |
| **Lemon wedges** |

Soak chick peas in plenty of cold water for several hours, then drain and rinse. Put into a saucepan, cover with cold water and simmer for 1-1½ hours until tender, then drain, keeping the cooking water. Either pass chick peas through a vegetable mill then mix in half the olive oil and all the other ingredients, or use a liquidizer, putting chick peas in the goblet with half the olive oil, garlic, lemon juice, sesame cream and some salt and blending to a smooth, fairly thick purée. You may need to add some cooking liquid to make a nice creamy consistency. Chill the *hummus* then serve on a flat dish with the rest of the olive oil spooned over the top and a good sprinkling of paprika. Garnish with lemon wedges. If serving as a starter, however, it is easier to put individual portions on medium-size plates and top each with some olive oil and paprika. Serve with extra olive oil and plenty of soft wholewheat bread or pitta bread.

**Approx. preparation and cooking time (not including soaking):** 1½ hours.

# Mushroom Tartlets
## Pastry

| |
|---|
| 100g (4 oz) vegetable margarine |
| 200g (8 oz) wholewheat flour |
| Pinch sea salt |
| Cold water to mix |

## Filling

| |
|---|
| 1 small onion, finely chopped |
| 1 clove garlic, crushed |
| 1 tbsp olive oil |
| 175g (6 oz) button mushrooms, finely chopped |
| 2 free-range eggs |
| 150ml (¼ pt) yoghurt |
| 1 dsp chives or chopped parsley |
| Sea salt; freshly ground black pepper |

Rub margarine into flour and salt until mixture resembles fine breadcrumbs, mix into smooth soft dough with a little cold water. Chill for 15 minutes. Meanwhile prepare filling. Sauté onion and garlic in oil for 5 minutes without browning. Stir in mushrooms and cook for 3 minutes. Remove from heat and set aside. Cut pastry dough into 4 and roll each out into round to fit individual tartlet tins. Line with pastry and bake blind for 10 minutes at 400°F (200°C) gas mark 6. Remove from oven, turn down heat to 350°F (180°C) gas mark 4. Beat together eggs and yoghurt, season and stir into mushroom mixture. Pour into tins. Bake for 25 minutes, until firm to the touch.

**Approx. preparation and cooking time:** 1 hour.

# Coconut Cream Dip

| |
|---|
| 25g (1 oz) dessicated coconut |
| 225g (8 oz) carton cottage cheese |
| 150ml (¼ pt) single cream or top of the milk |
| ½ tsp honey |

Liquidize all the ingredients together. Can be served as a dip with crisp celery, apple, pear and pineapple pieces and grapes. Also makes a good dressing for fruit salads.

**Approx. preparation time:** 5 minutes.

# Salads and Dressings

Forget the humble lettuce leaf, tomato and cucumber conception of a salad and let your imagination run riot with combinations of vegetables (raw and cooked), sprouted beans and seeds, fruit (fresh and dried), pulses and other protein sources like cheese, nuts and seeds, with a variety of dressings. Salads can be meals in themselves with the addition of cooked beans, wholewheat pasta, brown rice or wholewheat bread whilst smaller portions make excellent starters or sandwich fillings. For economy, base salads on whatever seasonal vegetables and fruit are available and don't forget that chopped fresh green herbs add delicious flavour and colour contrast, too.

## Chicory Flower Salad

| |
|---|
| **225g (8 oz) curd cheese** |
| **125g (4 oz) finely grated orange-coloured cheese** |
| **1 tbsp tomato ketchup or purée** |
| **½ tsp paprika pepper** |
| **Sea salt; freshly ground blackpepper** |
| **3 heads of chicory, washed and broken into leaves** |
| **2 carrots, scraped and cut into rings** |
| **Juice of 1 lemon** |
| **2 tbsp olive oil** |

Mix together curd cheese, grated cheese, tomato ketchup or purée and paprika pepper; season. Heap this mixture up in the centre of a flat serving dish. Stick the chicory all round the edge of this in two layers, like petals. Toss the carrot slices in lemon juice and arrange over top of the cheese mixture; spoon the oil over the carrot.

This salad can be eaten with the fingers, using the chicory to scoop up the dip.

**Approx. preparation time:** 10 minutes.

# ☆ Special Rice Salad ☆

| |
|---|
| **1 medium-sized aubergine** |
| **Sea salt** |
| **225g (8 oz) long grain brown rice** |
| **400ml (¾ pt) water** |
| **2 onions, peeled and chopped** |
| **3-4 garlic cloves, peeled and crushed** |
| **1 tbsp sunflower oil** |
| **1 red pepper** |
| **225g (8 oz) button mushrooms, washed** |
| **4 tomatoes, peeled and chopped** |
| **1 tbsp wine vinegar** |
| **Tabasco sauce; freshly ground black pepper** |
| **125g (4 oz) cashew nuts (roasted on dry baking sheet in moderate oven until golden)** |

Wash aubergine and remove stalk. Cut flesh into dice, sprinkle with salt and leave on one side for bitter juices to be drawn out. Put rice and water into saucepan with 1 tsp salt; bring to boil, then cover and leave to cook over very gentle heat for 45 minutes until rice is tender.

While rice is cooking, fry onion and garlic in oil for 10 minutes until softened. Halve, de-seed and chop pepper, then add to onions. Squeeze aubergines then rinse under cold water and pat dry; add to onion mixture. Cook for 5-10 minutes until aubergine and pepper are almost tender, then add mushrooms and fry for 2 minutes more just to cook mushrooms briefly. Stir in tomatoes then remove from heat.

When rice is cooked, turn into large bowl, add vegetables and mix lightly with fork. Stir in wine vinegar, a few drops of tabasco, a good grinding of pepper and a little more salt if necessary. Cool and stir in cashew nuts just before serving.

Serve with lettuce and watercress or a mixed green salad for a complete main course.

**Approx. preparation and cooking time:** 50 minutes.

# Citrus Watercress Salad

| |
|---|
| **225g (8 oz) cooked brown rice** |
| **2 oranges** |
| **1 grapefruit** |
| **½ tsp grated nutmeg** |
| **25g (1 oz) chopped almonds** |
| **4 bunches watercress** |

Section citrus fruits and chop into small pieces. Combine rice, almonds and spice in a bowl and carefully mix in fruit, taking care not to break it. Serve on a bed of watercress.

**Approx. preparation time:** 10 minutes.


# Salade Niçoise

| |
|---|
| **1 large lettuce** |
| **1 medium-sized onion, peeled** |
| **450g (1 lb) firm tomatoes** |
| **5 hard boiled eggs\*** |
| **450g (1 lb) French beans, cooked** |
| **12 black olives** |
| **2 tbsp fresh parsley, chopped** |
| **2 tbsp best quality olive oil** |
| **1 tbsp red wine vinegar** |
| **Sea salt, freshly ground black pepper** |

Line a flat serving dish with the lettuce. Thinly slice onion, quarter tomatoes and eggs, cut French beans into even-sized lengths. Put vegetables and eggs into bowl and add olives, parsley, oil and vinegar with a little salt and pepper. Mix gently to coat everything with dressing. Heap salad on top of lettuce and serve as soon as possible.

Serve with warm crunchy wholewheat rolls.

**Approx. preparation time:** 10 minutes.

\*Eggs can be replaced by drained butter beans using 100g (3-4 oz) dry weight or a 425g (15 oz) can, or 125g (4 oz) roasted cashew nuts.

# Fennel, Carrot and Spring Onion Salad

| |
|---|
| 2 tbsp lemon juice |
| 2 tbsp sunflower oil |
| Sea salt; freshly ground black pepper |
| 1 large bulb fennel |
| 225g (8 oz) carrots, scraped and coarsely grated |
| 4 spring onions, chopped |

Put lemon juice and sunflower oil into a large bowl with a little salt and pepper and mix to make a simple dressing. Wash and slice the fennel, trimming off any tough outer layers but keeping feathery green top: chop these green bits and add to dressing in the bowl, along with the sliced fennel, grated carrots and spring onions. Mix well. This salad improves with standing: leave for up to 2 hours, turning the ingredients from time to time.

**Approx. preparation time:** 10 minutes.

## Variation

Raisins and flaked almonds can be added for a pleasant change.

# Coleslaw

| |
|---|
| **350g (12 oz) white cabbage** |
| **1 large carrot** |
| **1 small onion** |
| **50g (2 oz) sultanas** |
| **3 rounded tbsp mayonnaise** |
| **Sea salt; freshly ground black pepper** |

Wash and shred cabbage; scrape and coarsely grate carrot, peel and finely slice the onion. Put them in a large bowl with the sultanas, mayonnaise, salt and pepper to taste and mix well. Cover and leave for 2-3 hours before serving if possible to allow vegetables to soften and flavours to blend.

The mayonnaise can be replaced by natural yoghurt for fewer calories, if preferred.

**Approx. preparation time:** 10 minutes.

# Greek Salad

| |
|---|
| **1 cucumber, peeled and cut into chunky dice** |
| **450g (1 lb) firm tomatoes, cut into chunky pieces** |
| **1 medium-sized onion, peeled and cut into rings** |
| **75-100g (3-4 oz) black olives** |
| **Sea salt; freshly ground black pepper** |
| **125g (4 oz) white cabbage, shredded** |
| **125g (4 oz) feta cheese, or white Cheshire or Wensleydale** |

## Dressing

| |
|---|
| **4 tbsp olive oil** |
| **1 tbsp wine vinegar** |

Put cucumber, tomato, onion and olives into a bowl with some salt and pepper and mix. Divide the cabbage between 4 plates, spreading it out into an even layer, then spoon the cucumber mixture on top and crumble the cheese over that. Combine the oil and vinegar and spoon over the salads just before serving.

**Approx. preparation time:** 10-15 minutes.

# Pasta Salad

**175g (6 oz) wholewheat pasta rings**
**Sea salt**
**1 tbsp wine vinegar**
**4 tbsp olive oil**
**1 large clove garlic, peeled and crushed**
**Freshly ground black pepper**
**1 ripe avocado**
**Juice of 1 small lemon**
**125g (4 oz) firm tomatoes, sliced**
**125g (4 oz) firm white button mushrooms,**
**wiped and sliced**
**6 spring onions, washed, trimmed and chopped**

Cook pasta in boiling salted water until just tender. Drain well.
Mix the vinegar, oil, garlic and some salt and pepper in a large
bowl, add the pasta and turn gently with a spoon. Cool, stirring
from time to time.

Just before salad is required, peel and slice avocado and mix
with lemon juice. Add to the pasta together with the remaining
ingredients.

Serve this complete-meal salad with grated cheese or a
wedge of Brie and some wholewheat bread.

**Approx. preparation and cooking time:** 25 minutes.

# Carrot and Alfalfa Salad

**2 carrots**
**Handful of alfalfa sprouts**
**½ pear**
**½ lemon**

Shred carrots coarsely, cube washed pear and turn both
immediately in lemon juice. Add the alfalfa sprouts and a
suitable salad dressing.

**Approx. preparation time:** 5 minutes.

# Red Cabbage Salad with Celery, Apples and Chestnuts

| |
|---|
| 450g (1 lb) red cabbage |
| 1 tbsp wine vinegar |
| 2 tbsp sunflower oil |
| Sea salt; freshly ground black pepper |
| 2 sweet eating apples, cored and diced |
| 1 celery heart, washed and sliced |
| 125g (4 oz) cooked chestnuts, halved or quartered |
| 50g (2 oz) raisins |

Wash the cabbage and shred finely or grate coarsely. Put the vinegar and oil into a large bowl with some salt and pepper and stir together. Then add the cabbage, apples, celery, chestnuts and raisins and mix well. This salad can be made an hour or so ahead of time; it keeps well and the cabbage will become softer.

The chestnuts give an unusual touch to this salad which is delicious in autumn with the first of the red cabbage and celery. Serve with jacket-baked potatoes, filled with soured cream, cottage cheese or fromage blanc for a complete meal.

**Approx. preparation time:** 10 minutes.

# Waldorf Salad

| |
|---|
| **2 celery hearts, washed and diced** |
| **4 large ripe eating apples, diced** |
| **3 tbsp natural yoghurt** |
| **3 tbsp mayonnaise** |
| **Sea salt** |
| **50g (2 oz) shelled walnuts, roughly chopped** |
| **1 bunch watercress, washed and drained** |
| **A little paprika pepper (opt.)** |

Put the celery and apple into a bowl and add the yoghurt, mayonnaise and a little salt. Mix well. Spoon the mixture into a serving dish, scatter the walnuts on top and tuck the watercress around the edge. Sprinkle a little watercress on top for an extra touch of colour if liked.

This salad goes well with cheese dishes and looks good served with some fresh green watercress.

**Approx. preparation time:** 10 minutes.

# Curried Yoghurt Mayonnaise

| |
|---|
| *Makes about 375ml, ½ pt and serves 6-8* |
| **1 tbsp oil** |
| **1 small onion, peeled and finely chopped** |
| **2 tsp curry powder** |
| **1 tsp tomato paste** |
| **1 tsp honey** |
| **6 tbsp red wine** |
| **150g (5 oz) natural yoghurt** |
| **150g (5 oz) fromage blanc** |
| **Sea salt; freshly ground black pepper** |

Heat oil in small saucepan and gently fry onion until tender — 10 minutes. Stir in curry powder, tomato paste, honey and wine and bubble over high heat until liquid has reduced to a thick syrup. Remove from heat and leave to get completely cold. Sieve and add the yoghurt and fromage blanc or liquidize them all together to a creamy consistency. Season with salt and pepper.

This dressing goes well with hardboiled eggs, bean salads and rice or lentil fritters.

**Approx. preparation and cooking time:** 20 minutes.

# Dressings

## ☆ Walnut and Almond Dressing ☆

| |
|---|
| 25g (1 oz) walnuts |
| 25g (1 oz) almonds — whole, flaked or blanched |
| 50g (2 oz) carrot, roughly chopped |
| 2 tbsp cold-pressed olive oil |
| 4 tbsp water |
| 1 tbsp wine vinegar |
| 1 tsp chopped fresh rosemary, thyme or marjoram |
| Sea salt; freshly ground black pepper |

Put all the ingredients into a blender or food processor and whizz to a cream. Delicious poured over green salad or with hot wholewheat pasta.

**Approx. preparation time:** 5 minutes.

## Vinaigrette

| |
|---|
| 1 tbsp wine vinegar, preferably red |
| 3-4 tbsp best quality olive oil |
| Sea salt; freshly ground black pepper |

Mix everything together, adding plenty of seasoning. Chopped fresh herbs, a little mustard and a dash of sugar can be added to vary the flavour.

**Approx. preparation time:** 3 minutes.

## Lemon Mayonnaise

| |
|---|
| 4 tbsp mayonnaise |
| 6 tbsp fromage blanc |
| 1 tsp mustard |
| Juice of ½ lemon |
| Sea salt; freshly ground black pepper |

Just mix everything together to a smooth cream and season to taste.

This is a creamy, yet light and refreshing sauce which can be served cold with main dishes or used to coat lightly-cooked vegetables before topping with crumbs and grated cheese and baking, for an extra-special *au gratin* dish.

**Approx. preparation time:** 3-5 minutes.

# Blender Mayonnaise

| |
|---|
| **1 whole egg** |
| **¼ tsp salt** |
| **¼ tsp dry mustard** |
| **2-3 grindings of black pepper** |
| **2 tsp wine vinegar** |
| **2 tsp lemon juice** |
| **200ml (7 fl oz) olive oil or a mixture of olive oil and soya or sunflower oil** |

Break egg straight into liquidizer and add the salt, mustard, pepper, vinegar and lemon juice. Blend for a minute at medium speed until everything is well mixed then turn speed to high and gradually add oil, drop by drop through hole in lid of liquidizer goblet. After half the oil has been added you will hear the sound change to a 'glug-glug' noise and then the rest of the oil can be added more quickly in a thin stream. If the consistency of the mayonnaise is too thick, it can be thinned with a little boiling water or some milk.

**Approx. preparation time:** 5 minutes.


# Coconut Cream Dressing

| |
|---|
| **25g (1 oz) dessicated coconut** |
| **225g (8 oz) carton cottage cheese** |
| **150ml (¼ pt) single cream or top of the milk** |
| **½ tsp honey** |

Liquidize all ingredients together. Serve with fruit salads or as a dip with crisp celery, apple, pear and pineapple pieces, and grapes.

**Approx. preparation time:** 2-3 minutes.

# Main Courses
# and Sauces

Perhaps the section where those new to a vegetarian diet experience the most change in eating habits, it also offers tremendous scope for imaginative cooking. Vegetables have plenty to offer in their own right and, combined with brown rice, wholewheat pasta, beans and pulses, nuts and seeds and a limited amount of dairy produce, dishes can be almost limitless in their variety.

This section is divided into perhaps more speedily-cooked dishes for cooker-top and grill like burgers, rissoles and pancakes, and those which favour longer, slower oven-baking like loaves and casseroles.

Many of the dishes freeze well so you can cook double portions of family favourites, and flans, loaves and pizzas are tasty when cold and useful for lunch-boxes.

Don't forget that the drier dishes like burgers and loaves are splendidly complemented by one of the sauces, which add extra flavour, colour and interest.

# ☆ Nutty Brown Rice ☆
## with Vegetables

| |
|---|
| 275g (10 oz) long grain brown rice |
| 500ml (18 fl oz) water |
| Sea salt |
| 1 medium-size aubergine |
| 2 large onions |
| 3-4 garlic cloves |
| 1 tbsp oil |
| 1 red pepper |
| 350g (12 oz) button mushrooms |
| ½-1 green chilli, if available |
| ½-1 tsp grated fresh ginger, if available |
| 1 tsp coriander seed, lightly crushed |
| 2 tomatoes, peeled and roughly chopped |
| 125g (4 oz) hazel nuts, roasted on dry baking sheet in moderate oven for about 20 minutes until skins loosen and nuts are golden |
| Freshly ground black pepper |

Put rice in medium-sized saucepan with water and a teaspoonful of salt. Bring to boil then cover and cook very gently for 40-45 minutes until rice is tender and all liquid absorbed.

Wash aubergine and remove stalk. Cut into fairly small dice, put in colander, sprinkle with salt and place a weight on top. Leave on one side while preparing rest of vegetables.

Peel and chop onions and peel and crush garlic. Fry together in oil in a large saucepan for 5 minutes, stirring often to prevent sticking. Remove stalk and seeds from pepper and cut flesh into dice; wash mushrooms, cutting larger ones. Halve chilli and remove seeds; finely chop flesh. (Wash hands well after preparing chilli as juice can sting if it gets on the face or in the eyes.) Drain aubergine, rinse under cold tap and squeeze dry with hands. Add mushrooms, peppers, aubergine, chilli, ginger and coriander to the onions and fry for a further 5-10 minutes until all the vegetables are soft. When rice is cooked, stir gently with fork to 'fluff' it then mix lightly with the vegetables. Add tomatoes and half the nuts then season well with salt and freshly ground black pepper. Serve with rest of nuts on top.

Basil or thyme can be used instead of ginger, chilli and coriander and the rice can be served with a crisp salad and a tangy cheese sauce or sharp-tasting horseradish, lemon and mustard.

**Approx. preparation and cooking time:** 45 minutes.

# Vegetable Curry

| |
|---|
| **225g (8 oz) brown rice** |
| **2 large onions** |
| **1 clove garlic** |
| **225g (8 oz) fresh or frozen green beans** |
| **225g (8 oz) carrots** |
| **225g (8 oz) mushrooms** |
| **225g (8 oz) haricot beans (cooked) or red lentils** |
| **450g (1 lb) tomatoes** |
| **25g (1 oz) vegetable margarine** |
| **1 tbsp ground curry spices** |

Soak rice overnight then cook, adding salt to taste. Meanwhile slice onions thinly and cook in margarine. Crush garlic, add to pan with curry spice and cook for a couple of minutes. Skin and chop tomatoes, add to pan, stirring well. Cut rest of vegetables into chunks or slices, adding to pan with beans or lentils. (If using frozen green beans, add during last 5 minutes of cooking). Pour over enough boiling water or vegetable stock to just cover. Replace pan lid and simmer until all vegetables are tender but not mushy. Serve with the rice.

**Approx. preparation and cooking time:** 45 minutes.

# Buckwheat Pancakes

| |
|---|
| **1 egg** |
| **75g (3 oz) buckwheat flour** |
| **150ml (¼ pt) milk** |
| **Good pinch sea salt** |
| **A little vegetable oil** |

Sift flour and salt into mixing bowl and make a well in centre. Beat egg and milk together and pour a little into flour, then add remainder gradually. Whisk well to get rid of lumps. Put a teaspoonful of oil into a pan over medium heat. When oil is hot, pour a little of the batter into pan and fry as for pancakes, flipping over. These can be prepared in advance and kept in the fridge, separated by foil or greaseproof, then heated through in a slow oven.

**Approx. preparation and cooking time:** 15-20 minutes.

# Sprouted Alfalfa Cheeseburgers

| |
|---|
| **450g (1 lb) sprouted alfalfa** |
| **50g (2 oz) wholewheat breadcrumbs** |
| **50g (2 oz) grated carrots** |
| **1 small onion, finely chopped** |
| **1 beaten egg** |
| **2 cloves garlic** |
| **¼ tsp cayenne pepper** |
| **Pinch sea salt** |
| **1 tbsp soy sauce** |
| **4 slices of cheese** |

Steam alfalfa sprouts gently for 15 minutes and drain well. Combine with breadcrumbs, carrot, onion, crushed garlic, seasoning and sauce and bind with egg. Shape into round patties and bake until onions appear to be cooked. Place slice of cheese on each and toast under grill until cheese is just melted. Place burgers in toasted wholewheat buns and serve with green salad.

**Approx. preparation and cooking time:** 25 minutes.

# Nut and Rice Rissoles

| |
|---|
| **325g (12 oz) cooked brown rice** |
| **175g (6 oz) milled or finely chopped brazil, hazel or cashew nuts** |
| **1 tbsp vegetable margarine** |
| **1 medium onion, finely chopped** |
| **1 tsp sage** |
| **Pinch cayenne pepper** |
| **1 egg** |
| **Sea salt; freshly ground black pepper** |
| **50g (2 oz) wholewheat breadcrumbs** |
| **Vegetable oil for frying** |

Mix rice and chopped nuts together. Sauté onion in margarine until golden. Mix together all the ingredients except the egg, breadcrumbs and oil. Lastly, add beaten egg and shape mixture into rissoles — flat, round or oblong-shaped. Coat with breadcrumbs and fry very gently until lightly-browned on both sides, being careful when turning as they may tend to crumble.
  Serve with tomato or spicy sauce and a salad.

**Approx. preparation and cooking time:** 20 minutes.


# Potato Cakes

| |
|---|
| **450g (1 lb) potatoes** |
| **Approx. 150ml (¼ pt) skimmed milk** |
| **125g (4 oz) grated cheese, nuts (any type) or sunflower seeds** |
| **2 tbsp chopped parsley** |
| **Sea salt; freshly ground black pepper** |
| **50g (2 oz) wholewheat flour to coat** |
| **2 tbsp oil** |

Scrub potatoes, cover with water and boil until tender. Drain, cool slightly, then slip off skins with a small sharp knife. Mash, adding enough skimmed milk to make a firm consistency. Stir in cheese, nuts or sunflower seeds, parsley and seasoning. Add some more milk if necessary — mixture should be manageable but not too dry. Divide into 8, coat in flour and fry in oil until crisp on both sides. Drain and serve as soon as possible with salad or a sauce and cooked vegetables.

**Approx. preparation and cooking time:** 50 minutes.

# Potato Pizza

| | |
|---|---|
| 2 large onions | |
| Vegetable oil | |
| 225g (8 oz) tomatoes | |
| 150g (6 oz) mushrooms | |
| 450g (1 lb) potatoes | |
| Sea salt; freshly ground black pepper | |
| 150g (6 oz) grated cheese | |

Peel and slice onions and sauté in a little oil until tender, then add tomatoes, peeled and sliced, and sliced mushrooms, and cook until mushrooms are tender.

Meanwhile, peel and coarsely grate potatoes. Heat a little oil in a frying pan and press potatoes into this, pressing down firmly, and fry with lid on pan until bottom of potato round is golden brown and crispy, then carefully turn over, using a fish slice, and fry second side until golden brown. Arrange onions, tomatoes and mushrooms on top, sprinkled generously with the cheese and place under moderate grill until cheese is golden and bubbly.

**Approx. preparation and cooking time:** 25 minutes.

# Wholewheat Pancakes with Stir-fry Vegetables

## Pancakes

| |
|---|
| **100g (4 oz) wholewheat flour** |
| **Pinch sea salt** |
| **1 free range egg, beaten** |
| **300ml (½ pt) milk or milk and water** |

Sieve flour and salt into bowl, make well in centre, add egg and a little liquid, stirring from centre to sides of bowl. Add rest of liquid gradually and beat well before use. Lightly brush heavy-based pan with oil and heat. Pour small amount of batter into pan and tilt to spread batter over base, keeping pancakes as thin as possible. When set, turn gently to cook the other side. Fold pancake over and remove from pan. Keep warm until required.

## Sweet and Sour Sauce

| |
|---|
| **4 tbsp cider vinegar** |
| **4 tbsp water** |
| **Juice of orange** |
| **1 tbsp Demerara sugar** |
| **1 dsp tomato purée** |
| **2 tbsp Shoyu sauce** |
| **1 tbsp sherry (opt.)** |

Place all ingredients in heavy-based saucepan and place over low heat. Warm gently, stirring, adding more water if mixture is too thick.

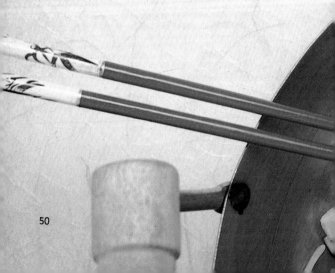

# Stir-fry Vegetables

| |
|---|
| **1 onion, sliced** |
| **1 leek, washed and sliced** |
| **1 clove garlic, peeled and crushed** |
| **1 green pepper, de-seeded and sliced into strips** |
| **2 large carrots, cut into thin strips** |
| **Few florets of sprouting broccoli** |
| **4 large Chinese leaves, shredded** |
| **4 handfuls beansprouts** |
| **1 small can bamboo shoots, thinly sliced (opt.)** |

Lightly brush wok or large frying pan with oil (sesame gives good flavour). Heat pan and add onion, leek and garlic. Stir-fry to prevent burning and to cook evenly. Cover wok and allow vegetables to cook in own steam for 2 minutes. Add green pepper and carrots, stir and cook for a couple of minutes. Add bamboo shoots and broccoli. Cover and cook for a couple of minutes.

Stir in Chinese leaves and beansprouts, continue stirring until heated through. Keep pan over low heat and take spoonfuls of mixture to fill warmed pancakes. Pour Sweet and Sour Sauce over and serve immediately.

**Approx. preparation and cooking time:** 20-25 minutes.

# Cashew Risotto

| |
|---|
| **1 large onion** |
| **100g (4 oz) carrots** |
| **1 tbsp oil** |
| **225g (8 oz) long grain brown rice** |
| **½ tsp dried thyme** |
| **450ml (¾ pt) vegetable stock** |
| **150ml (¼ pt) dry white wine or extra stock** |
| **100g (4 oz) button mushrooms, sliced** |
| **4 tbsp sweetcorn kernels** |
| **Bay leaf** |
| **225g (8 oz) courgettes** |
| **100g (4 oz) cashew nuts** |
| **2 tbsp sunflower seeds** |
| **Freshly ground black pepper** |

Finely chop onion, scrub and dice carrots. Sauté in oil for 2 minutes over low heat. Stir in rice and thyme, and cook for 1 minute until rice grains turn transparent. Add stock, wine, sliced mushrooms, sweetcorn kernels, bay leaf and bring to boil. Reduce heat and simmer for 20 minutes. Add sliced courgettes and continue cooking for 5-8 minutes until rice is just tender. Add cashews and sunflower seeds and heat through, reducing surplus liquid. Season with pepper, remove bay leaf and serve.

**Approx. preparation and cooking time:** 55 minutes.

# Speedy Burgers

| |
|---|
| **75g (3 oz) ground hazelnuts** |
| **100g (4 oz) wholewheat breadcrumbs** |
| **1 tbsp sunflower seeds** |
| **1 tbsp sesame seeds** |
| **50g (2 oz) carrots** |
| **1 small onion** |
| **1 stick celery** |
| **1 dsp oil** |
| **½ tsp dried sage** |
| **1 free-range egg** |
| **Oil for cooking** |

Put ground hazelnuts, 88g (3½ oz) breadcrumbs, sunflower and sesame seeds in a mixing bowl, stirring well. Scrub carrot and finely grate into mixture. Finely chop onion and celery and sauté together in oil for a couple of minutes (without browning). Add to bowl with sage, mix well and add beaten egg. Season with freshly ground black pepper. Divide mixture into 4, shape into burgers and toss in remaining breadcrumbs. Leave to chill for 30 minutes then fry in a little oil for 5 minutes each side.

**Approx. preparation and cooking time (not including chilling):** 20 minutes.

# Curried Rice and Cheese Fritters

| |
|---|
| **Approx. 450g (1 lb) cooked brown rice** |
| **(about 225g, 8 oz uncooked)** |
| **125g (4 oz) grated cheese** |
| **2 tsp curry powder** |
| **2 eggs, beaten** |
| **Sea salt; freshly ground black pepper** |
| **50g (2 oz) soft wholewheat breadcrumbs for coating** |
| **Oil for shallow frying** |

Mix together cooked rice, grated cheese, curry powder and half the beaten egg. Season with salt and pepper. Form into croquettes, dip each in rest of beaten egg then coat with breadcrumbs. Fry croquettes quickly on both sides in minimum of oil. Drain well and serve as soon as possible.

Good served with a crisp salad and natural yoghurt or yoghurt/mayonnaise dressing, or a tomato or curry sauce and a cooked vegetable. Recipe can be varied by adding 2 chopped hard-boiled eggs to mixture.

**Approx. preparation and cooking time:** 15-20 minutes.

# Crispy Filled Pancakes

## Batter

| |
|---|
| 100g (4 oz) wholewheat flour |
| 2 free-range eggs |
| 150ml (¼ pt) skim milk |
| 150ml (¼ pt) water |
| Oil for frying |

## Filling

| |
|---|
| 1 large onion, chopped |
| 1 leek, sliced |
| 2 large carrots, scrubbed and cut into thin strips |
| 50g (2 oz) button mushrooms, sliced |
| 75g (3 oz) savoy cabbage, shredded |
| 1 green pepper, deseeded and sliced |
| 3 handfuls beanshoots |
| Oil |
| 1 tbsp soy sauce |
| 3 tbsp water |
| Cornflour to thicken |

Sieve flour and add bran from sieve. Make well in centre and add eggs. Mix in with flour, gradually adding milk to make a smooth batter. Beat well for 4-5 minutes, add water and beat again. Heat a little oil in a small frying-pan and pour in just enough batter to coat base of pan. Cook for a few minutes, then turn pancake and cook other side. Slide pancake onto heated dish and place in oven to keep warm, or put on plate over pan of hot water and cover. Cook remaining batter into pancakes and keep warm.

To cook filling, put a little oil in a wok or large, heavy-based frying-pan. Add onion, leek, carrot and mushrooms and cook for 2 minutes. Add remaining vegetables, soy sauce and water and cook for 3 minutes. Thicken if liked with a little cornflour mixed with cold water. Divide mixture between pancakes and roll up. Serve at once with soy sauce.

**Approx. preparation and cooking time:** 30 minutes.

# Lazy Gnocchi

### Serves 4-6

| |
|---|
| **575ml (1 pt) liquid skimmed milk** |
| **1 bay leaf** |
| **1 onion stuck with clove** |
| **175g (6 oz) wholewheat semolina** |
| **150g (6 oz) grated cheese** |
| **1 tsp mustard powder** |
| **Sea salt; freshly ground black pepper** |
| **1 tomato, sliced** |

Put milk in large saucepan with bay leaf and onion and bring to boil. Remove from heat, cover and leave for at least 10 minutes. Remove bay leaf and onion. Bring milk to boil again then gradually sprinkle semolina over surface, stirring all the time, until you have a smooth, thick sauce. Let cook over gentle heat for 5 minutes, stirring often. Remove from heat and stir in two-thirds of cheese, mustard and some salt and pepper. Pour the thick mixture into a shallow ovenproof dish so that it makes a layer not more than 1cm (½ inch) deep. Top with rest of cheese and slices of tomato. Put under hot grill for 10-15 minutes until bubbling underneath and golden brown and crisp on top. Serve at once.

This can also be made into fritters, without the extra cheese. Spread mixture out about 5mm (¼ inch) deep on a flat plate and leave to get completely cold. Cut into pieces and dip each into beaten egg, then breadcrumbs, pressing to make crumbs stick. Shallow fry quickly on both sides until lightly browned and crisp. Serve quickly, dusted with Parmesan.

**Approx. preparation and cooking time:** 45-50 minutes.

# Oven Bakes

## Easy Pasta and Cheese Bake

| |
|---|
| **4 large onions, chopped** |
| **2 tsp ghee (clarified butter)** |
| **175g (6 oz) wholewheat pasta rings** |
| **700g (1½ lbs) tomatoes, skinned and chopped or 2 × 14 oz cans** |
| **125g (4 oz) grated cheese** |

Set oven to 300°F (150°C) gas mark 2. (If pre-setting it, time for 2 hours.) Peel and slice onions. Using a pan or flameproof casserole, fry in the butter for 5 minutes. If necessary, transfer to an oven dish. Put uncooked pasta rings in an even layer on top and tomatoes on top of that, making sure pasta is covered. Sprinkle with grated cheese. Cover and bake for 2 hours. Serve with a green salad. Wholewheat pasta and cheese protein combine to make a nourishing meal.

**Approx. preparation and cooking time:** 2 hours 10 minutes.

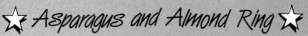
# ⭐ Asparagus and Almond Ring ⭐

| |
|---|
| 1 medium onion |
| 50g (2 oz) butter |
| 1 tsp mixed herbs |
| 1 tbsp plain flour |
| 150ml (¼ pt) milk |
| 1 egg |
| Sea salt; freshly ground black pepper |
| 225g (8 oz) milled almonds |
| 125g (4 oz) wholewheat breadcrumbs |

Peel and finely chop onion and cook with the mixed herbs in the butter until soft but not brown — about 10 minutes. Blend in the flour, then add the milk, beaten egg and the rest of the ingredients and cook gently for 2 minutes. Grease a large flat casserole dish or oven sheet and place the almond mixture on it in the shape of a ring with a hole in the middle. Bake in a slow oven 325°F (160°C), gas mark 3 for 1 hour. Remove from oven and place on a serving dish. Fill the centre with the asparagus mixture and garnish with roasted almonds and fresh parsley sprigs.

This ring may be cooked in advance and then filled with stuffing and heated through in a warm oven when required.

**Approx. preparation and cooking time:** 1 hour 20 minutes.


## Asparagus Stuffing

| |
|---|
| 100g (4 oz) button mushrooms |
| 50g (2 oz) butter |
| 4 tomatoes |
| 1 small can asparagus |
| Sea salt; freshly ground black pepper |
| parsley |

Wash mushrooms and cook gently in the butter for 5 minutes. Remove skins from tomatoes by immersing in boiling water for 1 minute then plunging them in cold water. Cut the tomatoes into quarters and add to the mushrooms. Drain liquid from asparagus, cut each stick into three pieces and add to mushroom mixture. Keep over heat until tomatoes and asparagus have heated through then season to taste and use to fill almond ring as directed after draining off excess liquid, then garnish with fresh parsley.

# Chunky Nut and Vegetable Roast

| |
|---|
| 1 carrot, scraped |
| 1 onion, peeled |
| 1 celery stick |
| 225g (8 oz) mixed nuts (i.e. almonds, peanuts, brazils) |
| 2 tsp yeast extract |
| 2 free-range eggs |
| 1-2 tsp dried mixed herbs |
| Sea salt; freshly ground black pepper |
| Butter and dried crumbs; |
| wheat germ or oatmeal for coating tin |

Set oven to 375°F (190°C) gas mark 5. Put all ingredients into a food processor and process until vegetables and nuts are chopped into chunky pieces. Or spread vegetables and nuts out onto large board and chop with an autochop, then put into bowl and mix with remaining ingredients. Line a 450g (1 lb) loaf tin with a strip of non-stick paper. Grease well and sprinkle with dry crumbs. Spoon nut mixture into tin, level top. Bake, uncovered for 45 minutes until centre is set. Slip knife round edge and turn loaf out onto warm serving dish. Good with vegetarian gravy made by frying a chopped onion, garlic clove, and 2 tbsp flour in 2 tbsp ghee until nut brown, then adding 400ml (¾ pt) water or stock, yeast extract, salt and pepper and simmering for 10-15 minutes, and cooked vegetables, or cold with a yoghurt dressing.

**Approx. preparation and cooking time:** 50 minutes.

# Quick Bread Pizza

| |
|---|
| 1 oval wholewheat loaf, about 450g (1 lb) |
| 2 large onions, peeled and sliced |
| 1 tbsp oil |
| 2 very large tomatoes, approx. 450g (1 lb) together or 425g (15 oz) can |
| Sea salt; freshly ground black pepper |
| Dried basil or oregano |
| 125g (4 oz) grated Cheshire cheese |
| 8 black olives |

Set oven to 400°F (200°C) gas mark 6. Slice loaf in half lengthwise and scoop out soft crumb (this won't be needed but can be made into breadcrumbs for other recipes). Fry onions in oil for 10 minutes until soft and lightly browned. Put the two halves of the loaf on a baking sheet and cover with the onions. Slice tomatoes if using fresh ones or drain canned tomatoes. Arrange on top of onions and season well with salt and pepper. Sprinkle with cheese and herbs and bake for 20 minutes until crust is very crisp and the cheese melted and beginning to brown. Decorate with olives and serve at once with a crisp green salad or an easily cooked vegetable such as frozen green beans or peas.

**Approx. preparation and cooking time:** 35 minutes.

# Chestnut Pie with Wholewheat Flaky Pastry

## Flaky Pastry

| |
|---|
| 225g (8 oz) wholewheat flour |
| Pinch sea salt |
| 175g (6 oz) unsalted butter |
| 1 tsp lemon juice |
| 150ml (5 fl oz) ice cold water |

## Chestnut Mixture

| |
|---|
| 1 diced onion |
| 200g (7 oz) cooked and puréed chestnuts |
| Wholewheat breadcrumbs |
| 1 dsp freshly chopped parsley |
| 1 tsp freshly chopped sage |
| 1 free-range egg |

## Brussels Sprouts Mixture

| |
|---|
| 100g (4 oz) Brussels sprouts |
| Knob unsalted butter or soft margarine |
| Sea salt |
| Grated nutmeg |

## Leek & Potato Mixture

| |
|---|
| 60ml (2 fl oz) vegetable stock |
| 60ml (2 fl oz) cream |
| 1 baked potato, sieved |
| 1 free-range egg, separated |
| 1 medium potato, diced |
| 1 small leek, diced |

For pastry, sieve flour and salt into bowl. Divide fat into 4 and rub one portion into flour. Mix to dough with water and juice. Roll out into long oblong on lightly-floured board, keeping ends square. Place another portion of fat in small pieces on upper two-thirds of pastry. Fold bottom third up over dough and fold top third down. Press edges lightly together to prevent air escaping and cover. Put in fridge to rest for 10 minutes. Repeat rolling and folding twice more, adding fat as before and ensuring folded edges are on the left and right. Roll and fold once more without adding any fat. After final rolling rest pastry in fridge for at least 10 minutes before use.

To make Chestnut Mixture: Sauté onion in smear of vegetable oil. Stir in chestnuts, breadcrumbs and herbs. Cool before beating in egg.

To make Brussels Sprouts Mixture: Steam or boil prepared Brussels sprouts in minimum of water until just cooked. Purée with butter and seasoning.

To make Leek & Potato Mixture: Warm stock and cream and mix with sieved potato. Beat in egg yolk. Whisk white until firm and fold in. Stir in vegetables.

To assemble pie: Line game pie mould with flaky pastry, reserving enough for lid. Place chestnut mixture in base. Spread Brussels sprouts on top and finally add leek and potato mixture. Place pastry lid in position. Seal edges, glaze with beaten egg and bake at 400°F (200°C) gas mark 6 for one hour.

**Approx. preparation and cooking time:** 1 hour 45 minutes.

# Lentil Lasagne

| |
|---|
| **175g (6 oz) wholewheat lasagne** |
| **1 onion, peeled and chopped** |
| **1 tbsp oil** |
| **125g (4 oz) mushrooms, wiped and chopped** |
| **425g (15 oz) can tomatoes** |
| **125g (4 oz) split red lentils** |
| **150ml (¼ pt) stock or red wine** |
| **3 large garlic cloves, peeled and crushed** |
| **½ tsp each dried basil, thyme, oregano and marjoram** |
| **Sea salt; freshly ground black pepper** |
| **225g (8 oz) cottage cheese** |
| **125g (4 oz) grated Cheddar cheese** |
| **A few breadcrumbs; a little Parmesan cheese** |

Cook lasagne in a large saucepan half-filled with boiling salted water; drain and drape the lasagne over sides of colander so that they don't stick together while filling is prepared. Fry onion in oil for 7 minutes, add mushrooms and cook for 3 more minutes, then stir in tomatoes, lentils, water or wine and crushed garlic. Cook gently for 20-30 minutes until lentils are very tender. Add herbs and season to taste. Set oven to 400°F (200°C) gas mark 6.

Put layer of lentil mixture in base of a lightly-greased shallow casserole dish, cover with some lasagne, followed by another layer of lentils, some cottage cheese, some grated cheese then lasagne; continue in layers like this until everything is used. Sprinkle top with some crumbs and grated Parmesan cheese and bake in oven for 1 hour.

**Approx. preparation and cooking time:** 1 hour 45 minutes.

# Red Bean Lasagne

| Serves 6 |
|---|
| 150g (6 oz) wholewheat lasagne |
| Sea salt |
| 1 large onion, peeled and chopped |
| 1 tbsp oil |
| 150g (6 oz) red kidney beans, soaked, cooked for 1-1¼ hours until tender or 2 tins |
| 225g (8 oz) can tomatoes |
| 2 tbsp tomato paste |
| 1 tsp powdered cinnamon |
| Freshly ground black pepper; dash of honey |

## For Cheese Sauce and Topping

| |
|---|
| 25g (1 oz) polyunsaturated margarine |
| 50g (2 oz) flour |
| 575ml (1 pt) skimmed milk |
| 125g (4 oz) strongly-flavoured cheese, grated |

Half-fill large saucepan with water with 1 tsp salt. Bring to boil then add lasagne, easing in gently as it softens. Boil without lid for about 10 minutes, until tender. Drain and drape pieces over sides of saucepan to prevent them sticking together while filling is prepared.

Fry onion in oil in medium-sized saucepan for 10 minutes, until tender. Drain beans, keeping liquid. Add beans to onions, mashing a little to break them up, also add tomatoes, tomato paste, cinnamon, salt, pepper and a dash of honey if needed.

Make low-fat cheese sauce by putting margarine, flour and milk into liquidizer goblet, blending for a minute then transferring to saucepan and stirring over moderate heat until thickened. Or melt margarine in saucepan and stir in flour in usual way, then add milk and stir over heat until thickened. Stir in half the cheese and season to taste.

Set oven to 400°F (200°C) gas mark 6. Put a layer of the bean mixture in a shallow ovenproof dish and cover with some lasagne; follow with another layer of bean mixture, then more lasagne and any remaining beans. Then pour cheese sauce over top and sprinkle with rest of cheese. Bake for 45 minutes until golden and bubbling.

Serve with a simply cooked green vegetable or a crisp green salad such as one combining watercress, celery and lettuce.

**Approx. preparation and cooking time:** 1 hour.

# Mushroom Loaf

*Serves 6*

| |
|---|
| **450g (1 lb) mushrooms** |
| **1 onion** |
| **1 tbsp sunflower oil** |
| **2 tbsp skimmed milk powder** |
| **125g (4 oz) grated nuts — Brazils or cashews or ground almonds for speed** |
| **225g (8 oz) soft wholewheat breadcrumbs** |
| **1 tsp Marmite** |
| **1 tsp mixed herbs** |
| **1 egg** |
| **Sea salt; freshly ground black pepper** |
| **Dried breadcrumbs for coating** |

Set oven to 350°F (180°C) gas mark 4. Wash mushrooms and chop roughly. Peel and chop onion. Fry onion in oil in a large saucepan for 7 minutes then add mushrooms and fry for a further 3 minutes. Remove from heat and liquidize. Add all remaining ingredients and season to taste. Grease a 450g (1 lb) loaf tin well with butter or soft margarine and coat well with dried crumbs. Spoon in mushroom mixture and smooth top. Bake uncovered for 1 hour. Slip knife round sides of tin and turn out loaf. Serve in slices with a savoury sauce and vegetables. It can also be used cold as a sandwich filling.

**Approx. preparation and cooking time:** 1 hour 15 minutes.

# Cheese and Onion Flan

| Serves 6 |
|---|
| 150g (6 oz) wholewheat flour |
| 75g (3 oz) polyunsaturated margarine |
| 1 tbsp water |
| 2 large onions, peeled and finely chopped |
| 125g (4 oz) fromage blanc |
| 1 tsp Dijon mustard |
| 2 eggs |
| 1-2 tbsp chopped parsley |
| Sea salt; freshly ground black pepper |
| 25g (1 oz) grated cheese |
| Dried basil |
| 1 tomato, sliced |

Preheat oven to 400°F (200°C) gas mark 6. Sift flour into bowl, adding residue of bran from sieve. Using a fork, work in the margarine until mixture looks like coarse breadcrumbs, then add water and mix to a dough. Roll out on a lightly-floured board and use to line a 20cm (8 inch) flan dish. Prick base and bake in oven for 15 minutes until well set and lightly-browned. Turn heat down to 375°F (190°C) gas mark 5.

While flan case is cooking, make filling. Put onions, fromage blanc, mustard, eggs and parsley into bowl and mix well. Season with salt and pepper. Spoon mixture into cooked flan case, sprinkle with grated cheese and a little basil and arrange slices of tomato attractively on top. Bake for 30 minutes.

Serve hot with cooked French beans and peas and tomato sauce or a salad such as one of carrot, apple, celery and raisin.

# Mushroom Flan

### Serves 6

| |
|---|
| 150g (6 oz) wholewheat flour |
| 75g (3 oz) polyunsaturated margarine |
| 1 tbsp water |
| 1 small onion, peeled and chopped finely |
| 1 tsp oil |
| 1 small garlic clove, peeled and crushed |
| 175g (6 oz) button mushrooms, washed and sliced |
| 125g (4 oz) fromage blanc |
| 1 egg |
| 1 tbsp chopped parsley |
| Sea salt; freshly ground black pepper |

Prepare pastry and make flan case, using flour, margarine and water in usual way as described under Cheese and Onion Flan. Bake at 400°F (200°C) gas mark 6 for 10-15 minutes until golden and crisp. While flan case is cooking, make filling.

Fry onion in oil for 4-5 minutes, stirring often, then add garlic and mushrooms and fry for further 2 minutes. Remove from heat and stir in fromage blanc, egg, parsley, salt and pepper to taste. Spoon mixture into flan case and bake for 30 minutes until set. Serve hot or cold with a salad or light mashed potatoes and a plainly-cooked vegetable.

# Aubergine and Tomato Casserole

| |
|---|
| 2 large aubergines (about 450g, 1 lb) |
| 2 large onions, peeled and sliced |
| 397g (14 oz) can tomatoes |
| 142g (5 oz) can tomato paste |
| 225g (8 oz) baby mushrooms |
| Sea salt; freshly ground black pepper |
| A little honey |

Set oven to 350°F (180°C) gas mark 4. Wash aubergines, remove stalks. Cut into very thin rounds, put into bowl and cover with boiling water. Leave for 5 minutes then drain. Put everything (including a glassful of wine if wished) into an ovenproof dish and mix lightly. Cover and bake for 1½ hours.

Serve with hot crusty wholewheat rolls, Bircher potatoes, brown rice or wholewheat spaghetti tossed in a little olive oil and seasoned with freshly ground black pepper, and a crisp salad.

# Hazelnut Roast

| |
|---|
| 2 medium onions |
| 2 eggs |
| 50g (2 oz) vegetable margarine |
| 100g (4 oz) ground hazelnuts |
| 50g (2 oz) dried wholewheat breadcrumbs |
| 1 tsp yeast extract |
| 2 tsp mixed herbs |
| Sea salt; freshly ground black pepper |

Preheat oven to 350°F (180°C), gas mark 4.

Peel and chop onions, and sauté in vegetable margarine for 10-15 minutes. Add nuts, breadcrumbs, yeast extract, seasoning and herbs. Beat eggs and add to nut mixture. Stir thoroughly, then bake 30-40 minutes.

Serve hot with vegetables or cold with a salad.

**Approx. preparation and cooking time:** 55 minutes.

# Mushroom Moussaka

| |
|---|
| **2 large aubergines** |
| **1 large onion** |
| **1 clove garlic** |
| **3 tbsp olive oil** |
| **1 tsp fresh chopped basil or oregano (½ tsp dried)** |
| **425g (15 oz) can tomatoes or** |
| **450g (1 lb) fresh, skinned tomatoes** |
| **1 red pepper, deseeded and chopped** |
| **175g (6 oz) mushrooms** |
| **50g (2 oz) soft vegetable margarine** |
| **25g (1 oz) 85% wheatmeal flour** |
| **210ml (7 fl oz) skim milk** |
| **½ tsp lemon juice** |
| **Pinch thyme** |
| **Freshly ground black pepper** |

Wipe aubergines and cut into 2cm (¾ inch) slices. Sprinkle with sea salt and leave for 30 minutes to draw out bitterness. Meanwhile prepare tomato sauce. Finely chop onion and crush garlic and sauté in 1 tbsp oil for 2 minutes without browning. Add herbs, tomato and pepper and simmer for 25 minutes. Wipe and finely chop mushrooms and cook in 25g (1 oz) of margarine until juices run. Melt remaining margarine in a pan and stir in flour. Cook for 1 minute, stirring, then gradually add milk. Continue to stir sauce to prevent lumps forming and give glossy sheen to sauce. Stir in mushrooms, lemon juice, thyme, and season to taste. Heat oven to 350°F (180°C), gas mark 4. Grease oblong ovenproof dish. Pat dry aubergine slices and fry in remaining oil until golden. Arrange some slices in dish and add tomato sauce, repeat and pour mushroom sauce over top. Cover with foil and bake for 30 minutes.

Serve hot with a side salad.

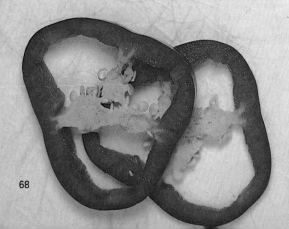

# Shooting Quiche

## Pastry Case (22cm/9 inch)

| |
|---|
| 200g (8 oz) wholewheat plain flour |
| 100g (4 oz) soft vegetable margarine |

## Filling

| |
|---|
| 2 cups any type of bean sprouts |
| 100g (4 oz) Cheddar cheese |
| 3 eggs |
| 400ml (¾ pt) milk |

Rub margarine into flour, adding enough cold water to form a firm dough. Roll out on large polythene sheet, turning both upside down over flan dish. Peel off polythene carefully and press pastry well into dish. Heat oven to 400°F (200°C) gas mark 6.

Thinly slice cheese, placing half on bottom of flan case. Cover with the sprouts. Beat eggs, add milk and beat again, then pour over the sprouts. Top with remaining cheese and bake for 15 minutes, then lower temperature to 350°F (180°C), gas mark 4 for a further 30 minutes until filling is firm and golden. Serve hot or cold.

# Sauces

## ☆ Mushroom and ☆ Soured Cream Sauce

| |
|---|
| **15g (½ oz) butter** |
| **125g (4 oz) button mushrooms, washed and chopped** |
| **150ml (¼ pt) soured cream** |
| **Sea salt; freshly ground black pepper** |
| **Paprika** |

Melt butter in a medium-sized saucepan and fry the mushrooms for about 5 minutes, then stir in the soured cream and salt, pepper and a little paprika to taste. Reheat gently, but don't let sauce get too near boiling point.

Good served warm and delicious with nutmeats, burgers and plainly cooked vegetables.

**Approx. preparation and cooking time:** 10 minutes.

## Tangy Cheese Sauce

| |
|---|
| *(Use 400ml, ¾ pt milk for a pouring sauce;* <br> *275ml, ½ pt for a thicker coating sauce)* |
| **2 tbsp unbleached white flour** |
| **275-400ml (½-¾ pt) skimmed milk** |
| **½ tsp dried thyme** |
| **2 tsp Dijon mustard** |
| **1 bay leaf** |
| **50-125g (2-4 oz) grated cheese** |
| **Sea salt; freshly ground black pepper** |

Put flour, milk, thyme and mustard into liquidizer goblet and blend for 1 minute then transfer to a medium-sized saucepan and add bay leaf. Stir over the heat for a minute or two until thickened, then leave to simmer very gently for about 7 minutes to cook the flour. Add the cheese and season to taste.

**Approx. preparation and cooking time:** 15 minutes.

# Parsley Sauce

As for pouring Tangy Cheese Sauce but leaving out cheese and mustard. Instead remove stalks from several sprigs of parsley. Put sprigs in liquidizer with the flour, 400ml (¾ pt) milk and blend. Use a generous amount of parsley for a beautifully-green and fresh-tasting sauce. Season well.

# Apple and Cranberry Sauce

| Serves 6 |
| --- |
| **450g (1 lb) sweet apples** |
| **125g (4 oz) cranberries** |
| **25-50g (1-2 oz) sugar** |
| **Ground cinnamon** |
| **Ground cloves** |

Peel, core and slice the apples. Wash and pick over cranberries, removing any stems. Put apples and cranberries into a small, heavy-based saucepan with the sugar and cook over gentle heat with a lid on for about 10 minutes, until soft and mushy. Mash fruits with a spoon or liquidize if a smoother sauce is preferred. Taste mixture and add more sugar if necessary and a pinch of ground cinnamon or cloves if liked.

This fruity sauce goes well with nut roasts.

**Approx. preparation and cooking time:** 20 minutes.

# Desserts

Although fresh and dried fruit make ideal desserts — perfect convenience foods! — there is often a need for a more elaborate close to a meal, especially if the rest of the menu has been relatively plain and simple. If it has been a little light on protein, for example, you can make up for this with a judicious choice of dessert.

As a deliciously light summer dessert, very popular with children, agar agar (the seaweed-based jelling agent available in health food stores) makes an excellent and nutritious setting agent for real fruit jellies.

## ☆ Yoghurt Glory ☆

| Serves 2 |
| --- |
| 1 medium-sized banana |
| 125ml (4 fl oz) raspberry, blackcurrant or strawberry yoghurt |
| 125ml (4 fl oz) low-fat natural yoghurt |
| 15g (½ oz) toasted hazelnuts, chopped |

Peel banana and slice thinly. Spoon a little of the flavoured yoghurt into base of two tall glasses, then add some banana slices. Top with a layer of natural yoghurt followed by more of the fruit yoghurt. Continue until all the ingredients are used up. Sprinkle nuts on top and serve at once.

**Approx. preparation time:** 5 minutes.

## Raspberry Creams

| 225g (8 oz) fromage blanc |
| --- |
| 2 × 200g (7 oz) raspberry yoghurts (preferably real fruit with no artificial colouring or flavourings) |

Put fromage blanc and yoghurt into a bowl and mix together. Spoon into 4 dishes and, if possible, chill thoroughly before serving.

**Approx. preparation time:** 5 minutes.

# Apricot and Almond Flan

## Pastry case

| |
|---|
| 150g (6 oz) wholewheat flour |
| 75g (3 oz) vegetable margarine |
| 1 egg |
| 25g (1 oz) light brown sugar |

## Filling

| |
|---|
| 225g (8 oz) dried apricots |
| 3 tbsp apricot jam |
| 50g (2 oz) flaked almonds |

Soak apricots overnight, then simmer until tender. Rub fat into flour until it resembles fine breadcrumbs, then stir in sugar and bind to a soft dough with the egg. Line a flan case, prick base with fork, then bake 'blind' for 15 minutes.

Remove from oven and fill with drained apricots. Heat jam gently in pan and pour over fruit in flan case. Toast flaked almonds lightly and sprinkle them over the top.

Serve with whipped cream or plain yogurt.

**Approx. preparation and cooking time:** 35 minutes.

# Raisin and Nut Flan with Spicy Pastry

| Serves 8 |
| --- |
| 150g (6 oz) raisins |
| 150g (6 oz) wholewheat flour |
| ½ tsp allspice or ground cloves |
| 1 tsp ground cinnamon |
| 75g (3oz) polyunsaturated margarine |
| 1 tbsp cold water |
| 250g (8¾ oz) quark |
| 2-3 tbsp liquid skimmed milk |
| 1 tsp thick honey |
| 50g (2oz) flaked almonds |

Set oven to 400°F (200°C) gas mark 6. Put raisins into small bowl and cover with boiling water. Leave for 10 minutes to plump, then drain. Meanwhile make the pastry. Sift flour, allspice and half cinnamon into bowl, adding residue of bran left in sieve. Using a fork, blend in margarine until mixture looks like coarse breadcrumbs, then add water and mix to a dough. Roll out on lightly-floured board and use to line 20cm (8 inch) flan dish. Prick pastry all over then bake in oven for 15 minutes until lightly browned and crisp. Leave to cool while making filling.

Mix together quark, raisins, skimmed milk and remaining ½ tsp of cinnamon. When creamy, stir in half the nuts. Spoon filling into cooled flan case and smooth top. Sprinkle with a little more cinnamon and remaining almonds. Chill before serving and use sharp knife to cut.

**Approx. preparation and cooking time:** 25-30 minutes.

# Banana and Nut Rice Pudding

| |
|---|
| **275g (10 oz) short grain brown rice** |
| **50g (2 oz) chopped hazelnuts** |
| **6 pieces dried banana, chopped** |
| **Pinch nutmeg** |
| **6 cups skimmed or soya milk** |

Grease pudding dish. Preheat oven to 350°F (180°C), gas mark 4. Rinse rice in cold water and place in oven dish. Pour on enough water to cover and cook until rice is just tender and the water absorbed. Remove from oven and add nuts, banana and nutmeg. Cover with milk and return dish to oven until rice is soft.

**Approx. preparation and cooking time:** 2-2½ hours.

# Wholewheat Apple Pie

| |
|---|
| *Serves 6-8* |
| **200g (8 oz) wholewheat flour** |
| **100g (4 oz) polyunsaturated margarine** |
| **2 tbsp cold water** |
| **450g (1 lb) cooking apples** |
| **125g (4 oz) raisins, chopped cooking dates or sultanas** |

Make pastry: Sift flour into large bowl, adding residue of bran left in sieve. Add fat and use fork to blend it lightly into flour. When mixture resembles coarse breadcrumbs, stir in water to form a dough. Leave to rest while preparing apples — peel and slice, discarding cores.

Set oven to 425°F (220°C) gas mark 7. Roll out two-thirds of pastry and use to line a pie dish. Put in apples, then raisins, dates or sultanas. Roll out remaining pastry and use to cover pie, trimming edges neatly and decorating with rerolled trimmings if liked. Prick top of pie then bake for 30-35 minutes.

**Approx. preparation and cooking time:** 45 minutes.

# Apple, Date & Orange Compote

| 700g (1½ lb) cooking apples |
| --- |
| 125g (4 oz) cooking dates |
| 1 orange |

Peel, core and slice apples; cut dates into small pieces, discarding any stones. Scrub orange in hot water to remove any residue of sprays, then finely grate or pare off thin strips of peel. Squeeze juice from orange. Put apples and dates into a saucepan and add orange juice. Cover and simmer gently until apples and dates are tender — 10-15 minutes. Serve hot or cold with slivers of peel sprinkled on top.

**Approx. preparation and cooking time:** 25 minutes.

# Real Pineapple Jelly

| 1 large can unsweetened pineapple juice |
| --- |
| 2 level tsp agar agar |
| 225g (8 oz) can pineapple pieces (in natural juice) |
| Few drops pineapple liqueur (opt.) |
| Double cream |
| Angelica |

Put juice into a saucepan and bring to the boil, then gradually sprinkle agar agar over the boiling liquid stirring until dissolved. Remove from heat. Drain pineapple pieces and divide between 4-6 glasses sprinkled with a little pineapple liqueur, if using. Pour juice over pineapple pieces and leave until set. Decorate with double cream and angelica.

**Approx. preparation and cooking time:** 10 minutes.

# Apricot Fool

| |
|---|
| **175g (6 oz) dried apricots** |
| **350g (12 oz) fromage blanc** |
| **1 tbsp honey (opt.)** |
| **A few toasted flaked almonds or sesame seeds** |

Wash apricots well in hot water. Put in medium-sized saucepan and cover with cold water. Leave to soak for an hour or so if possible, then simmer over a low heat for 20-30 minutes until they're very tender and the water is reduced to a syrupy glaze. Cool, then liquidize to a thick purée. Mix the apricot purée with the fromage blanc, beating well until smooth and creamy — add honey if liked. Spoon mixture into 4 dishes — it looks lovely in glass ones — and chill. Serve sprinkled with a few toasted flaked almonds or sesame seeds.

**Approx. preparation and cooking time (including soaking time):** 1-1½ hours.

# Date Flan with Orange Pastry

| |
|---|
| *Serves 6-8* |
| **225g (8 oz) cooking dates** |
| **150ml (¼ pt) orange juice** |
| **200g (8 oz) wholewheat flour** |
| **100g (4 oz) polyunsaturated margarine** |
| **Grated rind of 1 orange and 2 tbsp of the juice** |

Chop dates coarsely, removing stones or hard bits. Put dates into small saucepan with the orange juice and heat gently until mushy. Cool.

Make pastry: sift flour into bowl, adding residue of bran from sieve. Using a fork, mix in margarine, orange rind and the 2 tbsp orange juice to make a dough. Roll out dough and use to line a 22cm (8 inch) flan dish; spoon in date mixture, smoothing level with back of spoon. Trim pastry. Reroll trimmings into thin strips and arrange in lattice pattern on top of tart. Bake for 30 minutes and serve hot with chilled natural yoghurt, fromage blanc or other low fat topping to give perfect contrast to sweet, crunchy pie.

**Approx. preparation and cooking time:** 45 minutes.

# Baking

Delicious and aromatic bread and scones to accompany lunch and supper dishes and a healthier choice for cakes and biscuits are included here. Useful for snacks and tea-time extras, too, and perfect as a basis for packed lunches, these recipes offer excellent examples of successful use of wholewheat flour which will encourage new users to experiment further as almost any standard recipe can be adapted, with perhaps a little extra liquid or fat as the flour tends to be more absorbent.

## ☆ *Sugarless Fruit Cake* ☆

| |
|---|
| **225g (8 oz) self-raising wholewheat flour** |
| **1 tsp mixed spice** |
| **175g (6 oz) cooking dates, chopped** |
| **150ml (5 fl oz) water** |
| **125g (4 oz) soft margarine** |
| **Grated rind of one lemon** |
| **3 eggs** |
| **450g (1 lb) mixed dried fruit** |
| **25g (1 oz) ground almonds** |
| **25g (1 oz) flaked almonds** |

Set oven to 350°F (180°C) gas mark 4. Grease and line a 20cm (8 inch) diameter deep cake tin. Sift flour with spice. Put dates into a pan with the water and heat until reduced to a purée. Cool. Put all ingredients except flaked almonds into a bowl and beat until thick and fluffy — 3-5 minutes. Turn into tin, sprinkle with almonds and bake for 2-2½ hours. Cool on wire rack.

The purée of dates replaces sugar in this recipe. It is lower in calories and rich in vitamins, minerals and fibre.

**Approx. preparation and cooking time:** 2½-3 hours.

# Wholewheat Bread

| |
|---|
| **675g (1½ lb) wholewheat flour** |
| **½-1 tsp sea salt** |
| **25g (1 oz) soft vegetable margarine** |
| **25g (1 oz) fresh yeast or 13g (½ oz) dried yeast** |
| **25mg vitamin C tablet, crushed** |
| **1 tsp honey** |
| **450ml (15 fl oz) water** |
| **1 beaten free range egg or skim milk to glaze** |

Mix flour and salt in large mixing bowl and rub in margarine.
Run water until tepid and measure 450ml (15 fl oz) into jug. Stir
in yeast, vitamin C tablet and honey. If using dried yeast follow
packet instructions. Stir mixture and when yeast has dissolved,
pour into the bowl. Mix to form soft but not sticky dough (may
need to add more flour or more water). Turn dough onto clean
surface and knead well for 10 minutes, adding extra flour if
dough becomes too sticky — it should be soft and pliable. Cover
with an upturned bowl and leave to rest for 10 minutes. Grease
2 450g (1 lb) loaf tins or baking trays. Divide rested dough in two
or into 20 equal pieces for rolls. Gently ease each piece out to
length of tin but three times the width and fold in three. Drop
into tin with 'seam' underneath.

Cover and leave to prove in warm place for 30-40 minutes
until double in size. Dough should spring back when pressed
with fingertips. If making rolls, shape each piece and space
apart on baking trays. Cover and leave to prove in warm place
for 20-25 minutes. Glaze loaves or rolls with beaten egg or milk
and scatter sesame or poppy seeds on top if wished.

Bake at top of preheated oven — 450°F (230°C), gas mark 8
for 30 minutes (rolls 15 minutes). Bread is ready when base
sounds hollow when tapped.

**Approx. preparation and cooking time:** 1-1½ hours.

# Carrot Bread

| |
|---|
| 225g (8 oz) wholewheat SR flour |
| 100g (4 oz) grated carrot |
| 100g (4 oz) Barbados sugar |
| 100g (4 oz) chopped hazelnuts |
| 275g (12 oz) natural yoghurt |
| Juice of 1 orange |
| 1 tsp mixed spice |
| 1 egg yolk, well beaten |

Preheat oven to 350°F (180°C), gas mark 4.

Mix together in large pan all ingredients except for flour and orange juice. Bring to boil and leave to simmer for 15 minutes. Leave to cool. Stir in flour and orange juice and bake in lined, greased loaf tin for about 1 hour. When cold, cut into slices and serve buttered.

**Approx. preparation and cooking time:** 1½ hours.

# Light Rye Bread

| |
|---|
| 450g (1 lb) rye flour |
| 900g (2 lb) wholewheat flour |
| 2 tbsp caraway seeds |
| 1 tsp sea salt |
| 50g (1 oz) yeast |
| ¾l (1½ pts) warm water |
| 1 tbsp honey |
| 50g (2 oz) vegetable oil or margarine |

Mix flours, caraway seeds and salt in a large bowl and set aside in a warm place. Add yeast to warm water, stir in sugar and melted margarine or oil. Whisk well together and put in warm place for 5 or 10 minutes. Pour yeast mixture into flour and beat to form smooth dough. Add a little flour if dough is too soft. Turn onto floured board and knead for 5 minutes. Clean mixing bowl and lightly grease. Put dough in it and cover, then leave to rise for 1-1½ hours in a warm place.

Grease four bread tins and divide dough between them. Cover again and leave in a warm place for a further 30-40 minutes or until doubled in size. Bake for 45 minutes at 375°F (190°C), gas mark 5. The loaves should sound hollow when tapped.

**Approx. preparation and cooking time:** 3 hours.

# Cheese Scones

| |
|---|
| **225g (8 oz) wholewheat flour** |
| **2½ tsp baking powder** |
| **½ tsp mustard powder** |
| **¼ tsp cayenne pepper** |
| **50g (2 oz) soft vegetable margarine** |
| **100g (4 oz) Cheddar cheese** |
| **1 free-range egg** |
| **Skim milk to mix and glaze** |
| **1 tbsp sesame seeds** |

Sieve flour, baking powder, mustard powder and cayenne pepper into mixing bowl and add bran from sieve. Rub in margarine. Finely grate cheese and set aside 13g (½ oz). Add cheese to bowl and mix in well. Add just enough milk to form a soft dough. Transfer to lightly-floured board and pat out to 1.5cm (½ inch) thick. Stamp out rounds with cutter and place on lightly-greased baking tray. Glaze with milk and sprinkle remaining cheese and sesame seeds on top. Bake at top of oven 425°F (220°C), gas mark 7 for 15-20 minutes until well-risen and golden brown. Cool on wire tray covered with clean tea-towel to keep scones soft.

**Approx. preparation and cooking time:** 30 minutes.

# Rye Meal Scones

| |
|---|
| **100g (4 oz) rye flour** |
| **100g (4 oz) wholewheat flour** |
| **35g (1½ oz) margarine** |
| **2 level tsp baking powder** |
| **35g (1½ oz) brown sugar** |
| **Just under 150ml (¼ pt) milk** |

Preheat oven to 450°F (230°C), gas mark 8.

Mix together flour and baking powder. Rub margarine into flour, then stir in sugar. Add milk gradually. Roll out dough and cut out fairly thick scone rounds. Place on greased baking tray. Brush tops with beaten egg or a little milk, if wished. Bake for 15 minutes.

**Approx. preparation and cooking time:** 25 minutes.

# Nut Pie Crust

| |
|---|
| **175g (6 oz) mixed nuts, ground finely** |
| **2 tbsp brown sugar** |
| **25g (1 oz) powdered dry milk** |
| **50g (2 oz) vegetable margarine** |

Preheat oven to 400°F (200°C), gas mark 6.

Mix nuts and sugar with milk powder. Melt margarine and add to mixture. Press into 22cm (9 inch) flan tin, covering base and sides. Bake for 8-10 minutes.

When cool, fill flan case with fruit (blackberries, raspberries, etc). Make glaze by heating gently together 2 tsp arrowroot, ⅓ cup fruit juice and 20g (2 oz) brown sugar until thickening then pour over fruit.

**Approx. preparation and cooking time:** 15 minutes.

# Nut Shortcake

| |
|---|
| 200g (8 oz) wholewheat flour |
| 100g (4 oz) vegetable margarine |
| 100g (4 oz) light brown sugar |
| 1 egg |
| 1 tsp cake spice |
| 1 tsp cinnamon |
| 2 tsp baking powder |
| ½ tsp sea salt |
| Jam |
| A little milk |
| 75g (3 oz) chopped nuts |

Preheat oven to 375°F (190°C), gas mark 5.

Rub margarine into sifted flour, stirring bran in afterwards. Add sugar, baking powder, salt and spices. Beat egg and add it to dry mixture, binding carefully. Divide mixture in two and roll out into squares to fit baking tin. Line tin with one layer of shortcake pastry, spread jam over, cover with other layer, brush with milk and sprinkle chopped nuts over top. Bake until firm in centre and cut into fingers when cold.

**Approx. preparation and cooking time:** 40 minutes.

# Digestive Biscuits

| |
|---|
| 88g (3½ oz) wholewheat flour |
| 38g (1½ oz) fine oatmeal |
| ½ tsp baking powder |
| Pinch sea salt |
| 50g (2 oz) soft vegetable margarine |
| 1 tbsp Muscovado sugar |
| 2-3 tbsp skim milk to mix |

Lightly grease two baking trays. Sieve flour, oatmeal, baking powder, and salt into mixing bowl, adding bran from sieve. Rub in margarine. Stir in sugar and enough milk to make a soft dough. Knead lightly. Roll out on lightly-floured surface to 3mm (⅛ inch) thickness and stamp out rounds using 7.5cm (3 inch) cutter. Place on trays and prick tops with fork. Bake in centre of oven 375°F (190°C), gas mark 5, for 15 minutes until pale gold. Transfer to wire cooling rack.

**Approx. preparation and cooking time:** 25 minutes.

# Victoria Sandwich

| |
|---|
| 100g (4 oz) polyunsaturated margarine |
| 100g (4 oz) Barbados or raw Demerara sugar |
| 3 eggs |
| 100g (4 oz) plain wholewheat flour |
| 1 level tsp baking powder |

Cream margarine with sugar until light and fluffy. Add beaten eggs very gradually, adding a little flour if necessary to prevent curdling. Sift together flour and baking powder, mixing in the bran left in the sieve, and fold in gently. Put into two 18cm (7 inch) greased tins and bake in a moderate oven 375°F (190°C), gas mark 5 for 20 minutes. Fill with sugar-free jam and top with a thick cream made from 125g (4 oz) fromage blanc, 2 tbsp natural yoghurt, 1-2 tsp clear honey (opt.) and ½-1 tsp extract of vanilla (opt.) beaten together until light and creamy and the consistency of whipped double cream.

**Approx. preparation and cooking time:** 30 minutes.

# Carob Brownies

| Makes 8 |
|---|
| 100g (4 oz) soft vegetable margarine |
| 2 tbsp clear honey |
| 50g (2 oz) molasses sugar |
| 2 free-range eggs |
| 25g (1 oz) carob powder |
| 88g (3½ oz) wholewheat flour |
| 1 tsp baking powder |
| 50g (2 oz) walnuts, chopped |
| 50g (2 oz) sultanas |
| Skim milk to mix |

Preheat oven to 350°F (180°C), gas mark 5. Grease a shallow 10cm (8 inch) square baking tin and brush with a little extra flour. Cream together margarine, honey and sugar until fluffy and beat in eggs, one at a time. Sieve in carob powder, flour and baking powder, adding bran left in sieve. Add walnuts and sultanas, fold in with a metal spoon, adding a little skim milk to give soft dropping consistency. Spoon mixture into prepared tin and smooth with knife. Bake in centre of oven for 20-25 minutes until just firm to the touch.

# Sesame Cake

| |
|---|
| **125g (5 oz) plain wholewheat flour** |
| **125g (5 oz) Muscovado sugar** |
| **1 tsp baking powder** |
| **Pinch sea salt** |
| **Pinch ground nutmeg** |
| **40g (1½ oz) toasted sesame seeds** |
| **50g (2 oz) soft vegetable margarine** |
| **150ml (¼ pt) milk** |
| **1 egg** |

Heat oven to 350°F (180°C), gas mark 4.

Sift all dry ingredients together and add sesame seeds. Rub in margarine; add three-quarters of the milk. Beat for 2 minutes at low speed if using mixer or beat well by hand. Add rest of milk and egg and continue beating well. Grease and flour 20cm (8 inch) cake tin. Pour in mixture and bake for about 30 minutes.

**Approx. preparation and cooking time:** 40 minutes.

## Topping

| |
|---|
| **150g (6 oz) smooth soft cheese** |
| **2 tsp set honey** |
| **25g (1 oz) toasted sesame seeds** |

Beat cheese and honey together. Spread over cake when cool, sprinkling sesame seeds on top.

# Lunchbox Snacks

Tasty and nutritious 'extras' to accompany wholewheat sandwiches, baps, rolls and pitta filled with chopped mixed salad, including beansprouts, soft and hard cheeses, egg, peanut and other nut butters, yeast extract, bean pâtés, sliced nut and bean loaves and other tempting ideas. Lunchboxes can hold quite delightful vegetarian meals — don't forget to include fruit juices in the summer, warming soups in winter, the occasional additive-free or natural yoghurt, seeds, nuts and raisin mixes, or little pots of rice or bean salad — the possibilities are endless.

## ☆ Savoury Flapjacks ☆

| |
|---|
| 150g (5 oz) rolled oats |
| 25g (1 oz) sunflower seeds |
| 25g (1 oz) sesame seeds |
| Pinch cayenne pepper |
| Pinch mustard powder |
| 100g (4 oz) Cheddar cheese, finely grated |
| 1 free-range egg |
| 2 tbsp skim milk |
| 75g (3 oz) soft vegetable margarine |

Lightly grease 10cm (8 inch) square shallow baking tin. Preheat oven to 350°F (180°C), gas mark 4. Mix together oats, seeds, spices and cheese. Beat egg with milk. Melt margarine, then stir into dry ingredients with egg and milk mixture. Mix well then smooth mixture into prepared tin. Bake in centre of oven for 20-25 minutes until golden brown. Mark into fingers and leave to cool in tin. (Makes 12.)

**Approx. preparation and cooking time:** 35 minutes.

# Cheese Shortbread

| |
|---|
| **200g (8 oz) plain wholewheat flour** |
| **Sea salt; freshly ground black pepper** |
| **Dash of cayenne** |
| **200g (8 oz) grated cheese — Cheddar or half Cheddar, half parmesan** |
| **150g (6 oz) butter or polyunsaturated margarine** |

Sift flour with salt, pepper and cayenne; mix with cheese; rub in butter to make a dough which will hold together. Check seasoning. Roll into sausage shape and slice evenly. Place slices on a baking sheet and bake at 375°F (190°C), gas mark 5 for 20-30 minutes, until golden brown. Cool on tins and store in airtight containers.

The same mixture can be rolled out and cut into long thin slices to make cheese straws — either way, these will add crispness and protein to a soft-textured meal.

**Approx. preparation and cooking time:** 40 minutes.

# Fruit and Nut Bars

| |
|---|
| **175g (6 oz) dates** |
| **75g (3 oz) dried apricots** |
| **50g (2 oz) dried figs** |
| **75g (3 oz) dried bananas** |
| **25g (1 oz) soft vegetable margarine** |
| **50g (2 oz) ground hazelnuts or almonds** |
| **50g (2 oz) ground coconut** |
| **2 sheets greaseproof paper 180cm × 280cm (7 × 11 inches)** |

Finely chop dried fruit. Melt margarine in thick-based saucepan over low heat, then add chopped fruit. Stir for 5 minutes until soft. Add nuts and coconut, blending well. Turn onto sheet of greaseproof and flatten with back of spoon. Cover with second piece of greaseproof and leave to cool then chill in fridge and cut into fingers.

**Approx. preparation and cooking time:** 15-20 minutes.

# Apricot Bars

*Makes about 22*

## Base

| |
|---|
| **100g (4 oz) vegetable margarine** |
| **50g (2 oz) soft brown sugar** |
| **200g (8 oz) plain wholewheat flour** |

## Topping

| |
|---|
| **100g (4 oz) wholewheat plain flour** |
| **200g (8 oz) soft brown sugar** |
| **2 eggs** |
| **200g (8 oz) dried apricots** |
| **½ tsp vanilla essence** |
| **50g (2 oz) chopped walnuts** |

Wash and dry apricots, cover with water in pan, simmer for 10 minutes. Meanwhile, combine flour, fat and sugar for base, mixing until crumbly. Press mixture into bottom of 30cm×23cm (12×9 inch) baking tray and cook for 15 minutes at 350°F (180°C), gas mark 4.

Prepare topping by chopping apricots finely. Beat together eggs and sugar until fluffy and mix in other ingredients except for walnuts and fruit, adding these at the last minute. Remove base from oven and pour topping over. Return to oven and bake 30 minutes more. When cool, cut into bars.

**Approx. preparation and cooking time:** 50 minutes.

# Flapjacks

### Makes 8
### 150g (5 oz) soft vegetable margarine
### 4 tbsp clear honey
### 25g (1 oz) raw cane Demerara or Muscovado sugar
### 225g (8 oz) rolled oats

Lightly grease a 10cm (8-inch) square shallow baking tin. Put margarine, honey and sugar in a pan and heat gently until margarine has melted. Stir in oats and remove from heat. Place in baking tin and smooth over top. Bake in centre of preheated oven at 350°F (180°C), gas mark 4 for 20-25 minutes until golden brown. Mark into 8 fingers and leave in tin until cold.

**Approx. preparation and cooking time:** 35 minutes.

## Variations

- Add 100g (4 oz) chopped dates, reducing weight of oats to 210g (7 oz).

- Add grated rind of one orange and 25g (1 oz) chopped almonds in place of 25g (1 oz) oats.

- Substitute 2 tbsp mincemeat for 2 tbsp honey.

- Substitute 50g (2 oz) dessicated coconut and 25g (1 oz) sesame seeds in place of 50g (2 oz) rolled oats.

- Substitute 2 tbsp molasses and grated rind of one lemon in place of 2 tbsp honey.

- Substitute half the weight of oats for muesli.

# Fruit Slices

## Pastry

**200g (8 oz) wholewheat flour**
**100g (4 oz) margarine**
**25g (1 oz) soft light brown sugar**
**Water to mix**

## Filling

**200g (8 oz) dried bananas**
**Juice of 1 lemon**
**Juice of small orange**

Preheat oven to 450°F (210°C), gas mark 7.

Mince dried bananas and add the fruit juice until mixture is soft enough to spread on pastry. Make pastry by sifting flour (add bran after rubbing in). Rub fat into flour lightly, adding an egg if you like shorter, richer pastry. Stir in sugar and add enough water to make a soft dough. Roll out pastry and use half to line a shallow baking tin. Spread with banana mixture, then cover with remaining pastry. Seal edges gently and prick top with fork. Bake for 30-40 minutes. Cut into slices when cool.

**Approx. preparation and cooking time:** 55 minutes.

# Oatcakes

*Makes 24-28*

**225g (8 oz) medium oatmeal**

**½ tsp baking powder**

**½ tsp salt**

**25g (1 oz) butter or margarine (melted)**

**6 tsp hot water**

**A little extra oatmeal to finish**

Set oven to 400°F (200°C), gas mark 6. Put oatmeal into bowl with baking powder, salt and butter or margarine and mix together lightly. Stir in enough warm water (about 6 tsp) to make a dough.

Sprinkle some oatmeal on a board and turn the dough out onto this. Knead lightly then roll out to thickness of about 3mm (⅛ inch), sprinkling the surface with a little extra oatmeal if necessary to prevent it from sticking. Either roll out the mixture into a circle and cut into wedges or stamp it into rounds using a pastry cutter. Transfer the oatcakes to a baking sheet and bake for about 15 minutes until firm and lightly coloured. Let them cool on the tray for a few minutes then transfer to wire cooling rack. Or serve warm and crumbly straight from the oven.

**Approx. preparation and cooking time:** 25-30 minutes.

# Sesame Balls

**100g (4 oz) soft cheese (preferably low fat)**

**50g (2 oz) dates**

**25g (1 oz) raisins or sultanas**

**1 lemon or small orange**

**½ tsp mixed spice**

**25g (1 oz) toasted sesame seeds**

**1 tbsp bran**

Chop dates and raisins finely. Mix with bran which helps to keep pieces separate. Scrub lemon or orange very thoroughly under hot water with stiff brush. Grate rind into mixture. Add spice and cheese, blending well. Roll into lozenge shapes (makes about 10) and dip into sesame seeds to coat sides. Store chilled.

**Approx. preparation time:** 20 minutes.

# Index to Recipes